Love
Coming
Home

Love Coming Home

Transform Your Environment.
Transform Your Life.

Jennifer Adams

BEYOND WORDS
Hillsboro, Oregon

BEYOND WORDS

20827 N.W. Cornell Road, Suite 500
Hillsboro, Oregon 97124-9808
503-531-8700 / 503-531-8773 fax
www.beyondword.com

Managing Editor: Lindsay S. Easterbrooks-Brown
Editor: Emily Han
Copyeditor: Linda M. Meyer
Proofreader: Michelle Blair
Design: Sara E. Blum
Composition: William H. Brunson Typography Services

For information about special discounts for bulk purchases, please contact Beyond Words Special Sales at 503-531-8700 or specialsales@beyondword.com.

Manufactured in the United States of America

10 9 8 7 6 5 4 3 2 1

Library of Congress Cataloging-in-Publication Data

Names: Adams, Jennifer, 1974– author.
Title: Love coming home : transform your environment, transform your life / Jennifer Adams.
Description: First Beyond Words hardcover edition. | Hillsboro, Oregon : Beyond Words, 2018. | Includes bibliographical references.
Identifiers: LCCN 2018012381 (print) | LCCN 2018013519 (ebook) | ISBN 9781582706917 (ebook) | ISBN 9781582706757 (hardcover)
Subjects: LCSH: Interior decoration.
Classification: LCC NK2115 (ebook) | LCC NK2115 .A33 2018 (print) | DDC 747.092—dc23
LC record available at https://lccn.loc.gov/2018012381

The corporate mission of Beyond Words Publishing, Inc.: *Inspire to Integrity*

To my sister,
Erica

Contents

Foreword

For nine years, my official title was "White House Doctor." That's an interesting name since I didn't take care of a house; I took care of the President of the United States and First Family who lived in that grand residence at 1600 Pennsylvania Avenue.

Despite, or perhaps because of, the pomp and circumstance associated with the White House, it was never really a home. For the president, it was a place of business, ceremony, and formal social events. Far from being a refuge, the White House was often an open target, both in the press and in physical threat. No wonder it's called the White House and not the White Home.

Being the White House Doctor gave me the opportunity to accompany the president on many foreign trips to meet with world leaders. During those official state visits, I got to visit famous dwellings such as Akasaka Palace in Tokyo, Buckingham Palace in London, Élysée Palace in Paris, and the Kremlin in Moscow. All were magnificent and imposing structures, but I had difficulty imagining how anyone, including a monarch, could feel at home there.

When Jennifer Adams asked me to read *Love Coming Home* and write the foreword, I was both honored and perplexed. What do I know about homes? As a US Navy brat who grew up to become a career naval officer, I moved more than a dozen times and spent most of my everyday life away from home. And when I was home, it was usually in government housing or a rental house close to the military base where I was stationed.

When I left the White House and retired from military life, I finally settled down in Arizona, where for the past seventeen years I have lived in five different houses. The longest I've lived in one house now is five years. Perhaps Jennifer asked me to read her book since she knew I was always yearning to create a home.

As a physician I know that having a *home* is good for your health. Children, families, and individuals thrive when they live in a setting where they feel safe, loved, and supported. So, when I think of the word home, I envision a place that transcends bricks and mortar. Home is a feeling you experience in a place where you belong. It is where you feel safe and comfortable to be yourself.

During one of my many travels, I saw a sign in a hotel restaurant that touched me so much that I wrote down the quote and kept it. When I was decluttering my home office the other day, I found the quote: "A space with your trace is a place of grace."

I'd like to add to that quote: "And home is that place." Home holds your energy and the energy of those who live with you in that sacred space. Home is deeply personal yet very public when we welcome others to share it.

In *Love Coming Home*, Jennifer beautifully describes what makes a living space truly a home. Her concept of home is the triumph of sanctuary over wood and steel. In this practical and resourceful guide, Jennifer shows you how to create a home or transform a house into a home. She draws upon her life journey, which grew from humble roots, and blossomed in her career as a successful interior decorator and founder of the international home décor company appropriately named Home by Jennifer Adams. Throughout the pages of this easy-to-read book, I can hear Jennifer's warm, engaging, and encouraging voice guiding and inspiring me to create my dream home. In many ways, Jennifer is America's home whisperer.

Before you run out to purchase paint, flooring, lighting, and furniture, read *Love Coming Home* cover to cover. Jennifer will teach you the power of Vision Boards to guide you in creating the theme of each room you decorate—before you start spending money. Don't have a lot of money to decorate? Jennifer knows from personal experience and can help you design the home of your dreams without having to win the lottery to pay for it. Struggling with mess and clutter? Jennifer has solutions for that. Disagreeing with your husband about displaying his motorcycle in your living room? Read this book. I wish I had done so five years ago, when my husband and I were building our first home together. We hired a helpful interior decorator and as a result, we got a beautiful home. But as I look back, I believe the process would have been a lot easier, more fun, and less expensive had I read *Love Coming Home* ahead of time.

You have in your hands a powerful tool that can help you create the home of your dreams, written by one of America's most talented designers, Jennifer Adams. Congratulations and enjoy the journey with Jennifer to home sweet home.

Dr. Connie Mariano, Rear Admiral, US Navy (Retired),
author of *The White House Doctor: My Patients Were Presidents*

Your Best Life Begins at Home

A House is made with bricks and beams,
but a Home is made from love and dreams.

Author unknown

Have you ever walked into a home that just feels right, but you aren't quite sure why? It's a gut reaction you have the moment you walk through the door—you're instantly comfortable. Inside, there's a fresh scent and a feeling of warmth and ease. The lighting is good, and the décor and palette exude effortless style and harmony. Everything is as it should be, and you feel right at home.

Then, is your next reaction something like this? *I wish I had a home like this . . . They must have hired a designer . . . I'd never be able to pull off something like this on my own . . . They must have spent a fortune . . . I could never afford this . . . I wish I was the creative type!*

Well, you're not alone. Many want a nice home but put restrictions on themselves, often without even realizing it. Subconsciously we may not feel deserving of dreaming big, of having the home environment we want, nor do we think we can afford to pull it off. We are held back by our lack of confidence, by not knowing where to start, and by believing that we're not creative.

What if I were to tell you that you, too, can have a home that feels just right? A home that is perfect for you. You might find it hard to believe, at first, but I assure you that it is possible, and not at some vague point in the future. You deserve to feel good in the home you live in right *now*; you don't need to wait until your next house. Why? Because home *is* where your best life begins, and you're already there. So let's get started!

A HOME TO THRIVE IN

This book will empower you by giving you the tools and knowledge you need to make wherever you live—be it rented, owned, or shared—a place you will absolutely *love coming home* to.

Good design is not some magic power granted only to designers or those who have big budgets. Throughout this book, I will show how you can create a home that is set up to help you thrive—a place that embraces your individuality, your lifestyle, and your budget. A home that feels right to you—all the way to your core. You don't have to wait for it, and it doesn't have to cost a lot of money. This book will empower you by giving you the tools and knowledge you need to make wherever you live—be it rented, owned, or shared—a place you will absolutely *love coming home* to.

From an early age, I learned that no matter where you come from, no matter what your resources are or what your current home arrangement is, you can create an environment in which you'll thrive. I now have the great fortune to be living in my dream home in a city that I love. However, my situation was quite different while growing up. I come from humble beginnings, in a modest home set deep in the countryside. When it came to decorating, and even basic necessities, my family needed to be extremely resourceful. For the most part, if something wasn't given to us by members of our family or our church, we had to make it. My mom even handmade our sofa! So when I wanted to redecorate my tiny room, which I tried to do frequently, I had to be inventive. And I'll never forget the satisfaction and joy I felt when my creative ideas came together.

I was always experimenting. Painting, moving things around, hanging posters and other things. I even tried tacking beach towels to the walls when I wanted a summer vibe and got a kick out of the cabana atmosphere. In an attempt for a new look, I once positioned my bed in a way that wouldn't even allow my door to close. That lasted about five minutes, but I learned from both my triumphs and mistakes!

My boldest move was tackling the yellow and green shag carpet that, though not stained or nasty, didn't fit my personal style. At all. My mom was diligent about keeping our home clean and rid of clutter. She would go to the local grocery store every six months and rent a machine to steam clean our carpets. All four kids would tag along, as a trip to the grocery store was a big outing for us. Once, while walking down the store aisle, I suddenly had an idea. What if I were to add dye to the water tank of the steam cleaner we were about to rent? That might be a great way to transform the shag carpet in my room!

I somehow convinced my mom to buy into my latest room-refresh idea, and she let me pick out my own box of dye. I found a fabulous shade of navy blue. Thankfully, for the sake of the rest of the carpets in our home, Mom made me wait until she had finished steam cleaning the entire house before she let me embark on my experiment. I remember that the anticipation was killing me—I couldn't wait to get started! When she finally turned the machine over to me, I filled the water tank, tore open the package of dye, and watched it cascade into the water and slowly turn it . . . black? Yikes! But that didn't deter me. I was taking the leap. Row by row I dragged the cleaner across my carpet.

At first the results were hideous: a shade of blue-black sprinkled amidst clumps of yellow and green. But I kept at it, layer by layer, and before I knew it, my carpet was transformed. It lightened up as it dried, and the black hue turned into blue. The variegated yellow and green was no longer visible; it had worked! (Well, sort of . . .) I was so proud of my masterpiece.

Such experiences instilled in me, at an early age, the importance of home and what improving it can do for your entire life. Transforming my bedroom boosted my confidence and gave me a huge sense of accomplishment. That blue color was so pleasing to my eye; seeing it brought a smile to my face every morning. My room now reflected my personality and style, and I was proud to show it to friends who came over to visit. Most of all, it was a space in which I felt at home—it was my sanctuary from the world.

I guess you can say that this was the start of my path into home decorating and design. My love for experimenting in my tiny bedroom and creating the best space for me inspired me to dream bigger—and to learn how to express myself, be resourceful, and go after what I wanted in life. Alongside my dreams, my family taught me to work hard and persevere in order to create my own reality. As a teenager I went from picking berries and doing odd jobs to cleaning houses with my sister every Sunday all throughout high school.

I was cleaning other people's toilets and making their beds long before I had my own bedding and home furnishings company. Not a glamorous way to start, that's for sure, but it made me who I am, and I am proud of my upbringing.

In my early twenties, after attending Heritage School of Interior Design, I dove right into decorating homes for other people. I loved it, but my confidence was low at the time. I guess that in my new big-city life I was a little intimidated, having grown up in such a remote country environment (our dining room table was a picnic table until I was seventeen!) Or maybe I had a hard time believing that people would find my ideas interesting. Remember, my experience up until that point was cleaning other people's houses or redecorating my own room. Who was I to make decisions about someone else's home, you know? In fact, the first design project I got, I charged only three hundred dollars to design the entire home. (If you have had any experience with designers, you know three hundred dollars might only buy you two hours of their time. Definitely not an entire home design!)

Because of a loving mentorship from Jan Springer, founder of the trade school I attended, I broke out of the limiting beliefs I had placed on myself. With the support of other mentors who came into my life (plus a TON of trial and error), my confidence and my design company grew substantially. I eventually assembled a talented and experienced team to help me realize my vision and went on to design extremely high-end homes, country clubs, hotel rooms, commercial spaces, and even airplanes.

My home design business has since evolved into an international home furnishings brand, and I am living my career dreams. I feel so fortunate to enjoy a life of abundance and fulfillment, doing exactly what I love—creating furnishings and content that inspires people to create their dream homes.

Vision Boards have been the keys to unlocking all my personal, business, and home dreams.

So how did I achieve my dreams? In great part, through the power of Vision Boards. Vision Boards have been the keys to unlocking all my personal, business, and home dreams. When I first learned about Vision Boards I read everything I could get my hands on about the topic. It was like a fire ignited inside of me. Using Vision Boards even helped propel my design business to a whole new level.

Vision Boards also helped me identify and clarify what a fulfilling life looked like to me. This visualization tool helped me see exactly what I wanted, and to break through limiting beliefs that were holding me back from dreaming big. Prior to this, all I really knew was that I wanted something "more." Through focused effort and consistent practice with Vision Boards, and a few other powers I reveal in my book *How High Can You Soar*, my dream life became clearer, more precise. Eventually, and in more ways than I ever thought possible, my dreams became reality. Using Vision Boards opened a path to a truly inspired life—and I'm going to demystify the process for you. I'll show you how to unlock the power of Vision Boards to help define, refine, and align your own home-related goals and dreams.

What Are Vision Boards?

To put it simply, a Vision Board is a place for gathering images and phrases that convey the emotions, accomplishments, experiences, intentions, and possessions you want to have in life—to help you visualize your goals and dreams. Seeing these meaningful images and phrases at least daily is key.

Through consistent use, I realized that the Vision Boards I created to benefit my personal life were similar to the design industry's Project Inspiration Boards, which I was using in my clients' homes.

Like these related visual tools, many principles of building success in our everyday lives and businesses are subtly related to the process of creating a home you love. And as it was for me, harnessing the power of Vision Boards will become a transformative experience for you, in more ways than you can imagine.

WHAT CAN YOU EXPECT

The tools and steps I teach in this book are a unique combination of my professional, hands-on experiences as a home designer, along with proven, researched methods established by transformational leaders in turning ideas into reality.

You will learn . . .

* How to expand your vision while clarifying and narrowing your focus on your dream environment through the creation of Vision Boards.

* How to make practical use of all those beautiful photos you see on Pinterest, Houzz, and many other digital photo outlets, and how to create a similar look and feel in your own home.

- The importance of having a strategy in order to avoid making costly mistakes that could keep you from achieving your intended result—your dream home.

- How to set an intention for every room in your home, which guides your decision-making process.

- How to put together your personal budget and an associated Projects List—a business plan of sorts for your home—that will ensure you have an actionable plan in place for accomplishing your home goals. (Don't worry; I'll show you how to break it down into manageable steps and help you pull it off wherever you are living right *now*.)

- How to reset and work through inevitable setbacks and mistakes, including trying to do too much all at once, holding onto objects that no longer suit your style or purpose, and so much more.

This book also addresses what might be holding you back from your dream home: insecurities, fears, and doubts—feelings that are common and can be resolved through clarity of vision. I will help you build confidence to make decisions, purchases, and improvements to your home without wasting money, time, or energy.

My hope is that not only will this book inspire you, it will provide you with the tools you need to assess what every room in your home means to you, both on the functional and intentional levels. Through the use of Vision Boards, this book will guide you in creating a well-thought out, manageable plan and a balanced aesthetic that you love—one that embraces your entire person.

I will take you beyond the obvious visual aspects of creating a pleasing home, into exploring other mind, body, and spiritual senses as they relate to your environment. Home is our sanctuary, our haven, our retreat—a little bit of heaven on earth. Home is where the heart is. I've experienced this truth so many times, in my own life and in the lives of my clients. And you can experience it too.

The power of home is real! No matter where you started out in life, you can have the life and home you dream of. First get clear on what it is that you want, and then learn how to turn it into reality. It's time to let go of all the reasons why you can't or shouldn't, and know that indeed you *can* and that you deserve it. You can have your dream home right where you are living today. You can create an environment you will always love to come home to!

PART I

The Power of Home

1

Creating a Happy Sanctuary

*When a flower doesn't bloom, you fix the environment
in which it grows, not the flower.*

Alexander Den Heijer

Have you ever stopped to think that you start and end each day in your home? Whether it's owned, rented, or shared, more than half of your life is spent at home. You might not have much control over the outside world from the moment you leave your home until the moment you return, but you can control your home environment, the space you occupy for so much of your life.

Your home has the power to help make every day a beautiful day.

Your home has the power to help make every day a beautiful day. The power to be a sanctuary from whatever is going on "out there"—be it at work or at school, in a line of traffic or in line at the market. You can create a home that always welcomes you back. Isn't that something to look forward to?

I had a client who . . . was a pilot for a commercial airline. He would fly all the way home from the East Coast to Portland, Oregon, simply to have one night in his own bed before flying right back to the East Coast for another trip. He claimed it reset him and gave him more strength for the week ahead. Being home—even for one day—was worth it, bringing him stability and happiness.

One thing we all have in common, no matter our background or income level or where we live, is that our environments, exterior and interior, influence every aspect of our lives: our health, our happiness, and our relationships. Everything! The home environment you create and inhabit is more than what you see; it's about what you smell or hear, the temperature around you, the light, the textures you touch, the ease of movement, the air quality, the cleanliness and elements of safety—or the lack thereof! It's also about things you only sense—the vibe, the energy, or the ambiance. Even the people you invite into your home have an effect on your environment.

Through your five basic senses, your environment affects your entire being to your core, your gut, or what we also know as your sixth sense or intuition. Simply put, your home environment matters.

So, why put off turning the one environment you can control, into an environment that soothes and inspires you, one you love coming home to each day, one that makes you smile the moment you open your eyes. It can be one that's healthy for you and your family, one that springboards your vitality, productivity, and positivity throughout the day, every day. And you can start creating it right now.

Even though our homes are important in our lives, many people don't respect, value, and treat them in that way; they put off making changes, thinking, *Someday, when I get into a better home, a better financial situation, or have the time, then I'll get my home in order.* Many anticipate or fear an eventual move or life change, so they just make do in their current environment. Many are paralyzed, not knowing where to start or feeling they don't have the ability to pull it off, even if they tried. Many truly believe that a beautiful home environment is only for the wealthy, or for someone who can afford a designer. These are all obstacles anyone can overcome. And this book will show you how. So why wait for someday when you can start today!

I had a client who . . . had been living in their home for ten years. This couple's house had a gorgeous setting with an amazing view, yet they still had boxes to be unpacked, furniture in disrepair, and an overall cluttered environment. *Someday* they intended to tear their house down and rebuild, or maybe sell it outright—after a decade, they were still unsure. Meanwhile, they were raising their family in an unsettled environment. They would apologize to visitors for the way their home looked, explaining that they were "in transition." Finally they realized how ridiculous this was! Once they acknowledged that putting off improving their current home was negatively affecting their lives, they stopped waiting for someday. They were then able to quickly and affordably make it a place they could enjoy *now*. Who knows . . . they still might tear down and rebuild, or even sell, but in the meantime they have created an environment they love coming home to, one in which their family can thrive.

I am a believer that simple shifts in your habits at home will make a big impact on your entire life. In preparation for making those small shifts, it's worthwhile to reflect on some aspects of your current space that will shed light on what home means to you:

- What do you love about your home?

- What do you not love so much?

- What in your home elevates you, inspires you?

- What in your home annoys you, frustrates you?

- What is holding you back from creating the home you want?

- What favorite memory do you have about a home? (It can be your own or someone else's home.) Why is this memory special to you?

- What excites you when you see other homes (in person, in magazines, or on Pinterest, and so on.)?

- What qualities are important to you in a home? (For example: color, lighting, coziness, openness, simplicity, a relaxing mood.)

Now let's take a few minutes to think through the start of your day:

- When you wake up in the morning, you feel textures against your skin. Are they smooth, soft, and luxurious—a delight? Or are they rough and scratchy? Or neutral, something in between?

- You open your eyes and see walls, a ceiling, the room as a whole. Does your waking environment make you feel good?

- When you step onto the floor, you feel a texture below your feet. Is it comfortable or slightly shocking? Warm and soft or cold and hard?

- You breathe in air, and what do you smell? Is it the fresh-cut roses on your dresser or the dirty laundry piled on the floor? Or maybe the preset coffeemaker is going, and the aroma is stimulating your senses?

- What do you hear? What sounds surround you? Do city noises jumpstart your thoughts and ideas? Or do nature sounds ease you into the day? Growing up in Gales Creek, Oregon, where we got a substantial amount of rain, the chirping of birds always symbolized sunshine and spring for me. Now when I hear birdsong in the morning, I wake up with a smile.

- You walk to the kitchen to get your morning beverage of choice. Will you feel smooth clean flooring beneath your bare feet or is it gritty or sticky? Can you comfortably reach your mug? Is there room on the counter to set it down while you pour?

INSIDER'S TIP: Is the sound of your alarm something pleasant? Or is it a blaring noise you can't silence fast enough? A simple change to your alarm sound will positively affect the way you wake up each day.

Your flow and movement through your home, whether unencumbered by objects or crowded with misplaced furniture or piles of clutter, also affects your attitude toward the day ahead. Tripping on clothing discarded in the middle of the bedroom floor doesn't do wonders for anyone's mood.

Where you shower, where you get dressed, where you exit your home—you may not be conscious of how these aspects of your environment support or impede your everyday life, but once you reflect on them you may begin to have a clearer sense of what is working and what isn't. You may even begin to note small shifts that could help make your mornings more comfortable and more pleasant—real solutions to help foster the best mind-set for your day.

Making Your Bed

I don't know about you, but if I leave my bed messy when I head out in the morning, my day doesn't feel quite right. The split second it takes to make my bed is a worthwhile tradeoff for the satisfaction I feel every time I walk by it as I'm getting ready for work. When I get home and walk into my bedroom to change into something more comfortable, my effortlessly styled, well-made bed suggests ease and relaxation. When I turn down its neat covers at night, somehow my bed feels cozier and more inviting. I swear I even sleep better!

In what has gone down as one of the best graduation speeches of all time, US Navy Admiral William H. McRaven shared his top ten lessons from basic SEAL training. Amongst his advice, he emphasized the importance of making your bed every day. I loved his entire speech, but especially this part.

"If you make your bed every morning you will have accomplished the first task of the day. It will give you a small sense of pride, and it will encourage you to do another task and another and another. By the end of the day, that one task completed will have turned into many tasks completed. Making your bed will also reinforce the fact that little things in life matter. If you can't do the little things right, you will never do the big things right.

And, if by chance you have a miserable day, you will come home to a bed that is made—that you made—and a made bed gives you encouragement that tomorrow will be better.

If you want to change the world, start off by making your bed."[1]

BEING IN THE MOMENT

Being in the moment—being present and mindful—enhances your life and your well-being. It's easier to be in the moment, and enjoy it to your core, if you're in an environment that supports who you are and the way you like to live.

Harvard University did a study on the health benefits of being in the moment, and proved that being in the moment brings you happiness! It states that people spend 46.9 percent of their waking hours thinking about something other than what they're doing, and that this mind wandering typically makes them unhappy. Time-lag analyses conducted by the researchers suggest that their subjects' mind wandering was generally the cause, not the consequence, of their unhappiness. The research was led by psychologists Matthew A. Killingsworth and Daniel T. Gilbert, who note in their findings: "Many philosophical and religious traditions teach that happiness is to be found by living in the moment, and practitioners are trained to resist mind wandering and 'to be here now.' These traditions suggest that a wandering mind is an unhappy mind."[2]

If your home is a constant frustration of clutter, ugliness, and imbalance, if it doesn't function well or just doesn't feel right, being in the moment can be extremely challenging, if not downright impossible. This type of environment provokes feelings of discontentment, anxiety, and unrest. It can cause your brain to wander from the here and now, which is not conducive to living your best life.

You owe it to yourself and your family to make your *now* home your best home, your sanctuary, a place where being in the present moment comes naturally and is a pleasurable experience. Your home environment has the power to reshape your mind, your heart, and your body.

Being present is valuable for creating your *now* home. When you are present in your home, you can better identify what's working and what's not. The next chapter will give you a useful tool to help tap into your ability to be present in your home.

Action Item

ASSESSING YOUR HOME ENVIRONMENT

- Make a list of all the things that cause you frustration in your current home environment, and of any home projects you need to tackle. Make this list in the order it occurs to you—no need to think too hard about it.

- Identify all the things that make you smile about your current home environment.

- Think through your day, from the moment you wake up to the moment you fall asleep. Follow your movements and activities, room by room, and don't forget the front entrance and the back door, the garage and the yard. Feel free to write down what you see, hear, smell, touch, and feel.

2

Delighting In
All Your Senses

*Never apologize for trusting your intuition—your brain can play
tricks, your heart can blind, but your gut is always right.*

Rachek Wolchin

In most areas of our lives, we focus on the things we see right in front of us—
the obvious. And no wonder, since sight is one of the most powerful and
influential of our senses. Because there is so much for you to see, the
visual aspect takes up most of your focus when putting together your home.
Your eyes might follow a neatly edged driveway to a flower bed gracing the
front yard, or maybe a neat sidewalk leads to your modest apartment door.
Once inside, there are intriguing objects, patterns, and shapes—eye candy
everywhere you look. You take note of the colors in each room, and the
ever-changing quality of light. You might have a window with an outlook, a
patio, or maybe a big back yard. Your home is full of visual elements, and it's

a common misconception to think that the visual experience is the only thing that matters when creating your dream home.

Often overlooked, these other senses—touch, sound, taste, and smell—all contribute greatly to that *love-coming-home* feeling.

However, four other senses (five if you've tapped into your intuitive sixth sense) are alive and alert in your body. Often overlooked, these other senses—touch, sound, taste, and smell—all contribute greatly to that *love-coming-home* feeling. The funny thing is, the elements that stimulate these other senses are not expensive to get right.

OUT OF SIGHT, OUT OF MIND?

Through inattention, your senses can grow dull over time, diminishing your experience of the world around you. Ignoring your sensory perceptions, especially in your home environment, is like shoving a pile of dirty laundry under the bed to hide it from unexpected guests. It's out of sight but not really out of mind, and you might even be able to smell it (ew!). The mess still exists, and it affects you every time you walk by the bed, whether you are aware of that fact or not.

Your senses are interpreting your world every moment of every day, influencing your feelings, affecting your well-being, and playing a profound role in the creation of memories. Even though you can't actually *see* smells, sounds, and tastes, you *can* open your mind and recognize how to delight in them every bit as much as what you see. Getting in touch with the four less obvious senses will greatly inform and support the visual elements you will establish on your

Vision Board in chapter 4, in turn helping you create a more authentic home environment.

If you're not used to paying attention, your senses might be a vague concept to you, but don't worry; I can help. I have learned how to readily identify the nature of these elements in a home. Using all five (or six) senses, I comprehend a great deal right when I walk in the door of someone's home, perhaps happiness and stability in an organized, well-functioning home or discord and anxiety in a chaotic environment.

Although I've often been called "the house whisperer," there's no magical power involved here, folks, I simply set my intention to have all of my senses fully engaged when I walk into any home. You possess this same power, and it's much easier to tap into than you might think.

JUST BE-ING

How many times have you seen a T-shirt or motivation poster that says, "Just Be." Or experienced someone asking, "Why can't you just *be*?" That used to be one of the most annoying questions anyone could ask me. I'd think, *What the heck does* just be *mean anyway? I practice yoga regularly, and I meditate, and I* still *don't get it*. As hard as I tried, I couldn't tell the difference between *being* and *doing*; to me they were the same thing.

Then one day, out of the blue, I met a random stranger, and in one minute he explained something to me that has forever changed my perception of *just be*, which in turn has helped me fine-tune my not-so-magical house-whispering power. A lightbulb went off in my head, my heart, and my being that day.

I was playing golf with my husband on a sunny afternoon in the Sonoma wine country. Now golf isn't necessarily my favorite activity, but when I get to play with my husband, I actually love it because it's great quality time together. I especially love it when we walk the golf course instead of taking a cart, turning the golf game into a nature walk instead of four hours waiting to hit a ball. The key here for me was in the walking part, the forward movement.

The flip side of walking a golf course is that if the group playing the hole ahead of you is also walking, and they happen to be slow walkers, a game of golf can turn into a five-hour torture session for a Type A personality like me, as you're frequently left standing around. Standing and watching the slow players ahead taking practice swing after practice swing as you wait. And wait. I've been tempted to hit a ball right up next to them to oh-so-subtly get them to move ahead, but that would result in getting us permanently kicked off the course, so for obvious reasons I hold back.

The day I learned to *just be*, we had a caddie with us on the golf course. Not that my game is good enough to warrant a caddie, but at this specific course it is highly encouraged in an attempt to speed up play. Which I'm all for! This day happened to be one of the painfully slow ones, and to top it off, no cell phones are allowed at this course. I had nothing to pass the time, or so I thought. I was stretching, lunging, pacing, doing all kinds of things, but being patient was not one of them.

As we were once again waiting on a hole, our caddie sensed my frustration and said he had something that might help me. It's a little secret that he said helps him tremendously, since he frequently has to escort older golfers who walk very slowly, and it used to aggravate him to no end. Silently grateful that I wasn't included in his "older" golfer group, I liked this gentleman even more, and my ears perked up.

What was this secret? At this point, I needed any tip I could get.

He asked if I had ever practiced Yoga Nidra. Yoga what? I had been doing yoga for over twelve years and had never heard of this type of yoga. Furthermore, how was I going to break into a full-on yoga pose out on the golf course? I still didn't see how this could help me out at all, let alone in this moment.

Come to find out, there are all kinds of Yoga Nidra techniques, but the particular one he taught me changed my behavior not only on the golf course, but in environments of all kinds, including the home. It's something you can do anywhere, anytime—and no one even notices. Now I totally get *just be*-ing. It has helped me so much! It's like this little secret I possess. Okay, not really a secret, since I'm about to share it with you . . .

Yoga Nidra is an activity involving the five plus senses. Activity in pursuit of *just be*-ing seems counterintuitive, but somehow it gets me to that *be*-ing state within seconds. Try it anywhere, even when you're waiting for someone, or standing in line. In fact, those are my favorite times. For situations where I used to feel annoyed or impatient, I've now learned to turn waiting time into gifted time during which I get to experience something special: *just be*-ing.

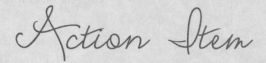

TAPPING INTO ALL FIVE SENSES

Here's how the Yoga Nidra version I learned works: you tap into all five of your senses and truly experience them—as if you have never done so before. Later we'll get into how you can apply Yoga Nidra to your home.

- *Tap into your sense of hearing.* Wherever you are, what do you hear? Try relaxing your "inner ear." I bet you never knew you could do that, but give it a try! Pay attention to every sound around you, from the quiet drone of a nearby fan to the breathing of another person in the room with you. What more distant noises do you hear? The intermittent hum of a generator, or is that a faraway airplane? Be present to all the sounds around you; listen and notice. You'll be amazed by what you hear, and by the realization that these sounds may have been there all along, without your truly noticing them.

- *Tap into your sense of sight.* Look all around you, and what do you see? Play I-Spy (inside your head, unless you want others to join in!) while you're waiting in line at the grocery store. Notice the rich color of the checkout clerk's hair (magenta?), the cute grin on a baby in the cart in front of you, the beat-up side of the counter, the unique lip balm that claims to fix your chapped lips, the elegant shape of the bottle of wine you picked up to enjoy at home. *I spy with my little eye . . .* the texture and materials used to put the shelves together in the aisle, the colors on all the marketing banners, and even the pricing signs. Notice all of it. Really see it, as if it were the very first time.

- *Tap into your sense of smell.* Sniff the air. What aromas, fragrances, or odors do you detect? You might be surprised to discover that you can smell more than one thing at the same time. Go beyond the obvious. Do you smell grass, water, food, smoke, flowers? Identify every scent that you can. Take it all in.

- *Tap into your sense of taste.* What flavors do you taste in your mouth? Is it fresh from toothpaste or stale with the lingering tang of the blue cheese you sampled at the grocery store? Notice your taste buds. Is your tongue clenched up against the roof of your mouth? Loosen it; relax your jaw and your tongue. Feel your taste buds come alive. They've been right there all the time, but we tend to forget about them. Even when having a meal, we're often too distracted to actually taste what we're eating. Now try tasting something with intention. For a moment or two be grateful for your taste buds!

- *Tap into your sense of touch.* How do your clothes feel against your skin? Your shoes on your feet? Is the sun warm upon on your face? How does the air itself feel on your skin? Are you leaning up against something? Is it soft or hard? Do you feel the fabric texture of your desk chair or the airplane seat you occupy? Is there a person nearby that you can touch? (I recommend only trying this when you know the person!) Hold hands if you can. How does his or her skin feel? Cool and dry? Warm and supple? Consciously experience this sense of touch.

Experiencing each of the five senses with intention is the key to *just be*-ing. You can do it in a matter of seconds or you can luxuriate in awareness for as long as time allows. It's amazing how quickly and enjoyably time passes when you try this. If you're anxious, *just be*-ing takes your anxiety down in a matter of seconds. I now practice Yoga Nidra anytime I'm waiting. It calms me, centers me in the present, fills me with gratitude, and brings me joy—every time. It took less than a minute to learn and I can call upon it at any moment, in any situation, and no one even needs to know. It's a gift I had within me all along, a "secret" that I've now shared with you!

In order to positively affect your environment as it relates to all five of your senses, you first need to be aware of what exists now.

In order to positively affect your environment as it relates to all five of your senses, you first need to be aware of what exists now. Practicing Yoga Nidra will help you tap into this power in a way you've probably never done before, especially in your home environment.

Try the Yoga Nidra technique right now. Be fully present, experiencing your home environment as if for the first time. Allow yourself the time to take it all in. Now let's go through all five of your senses as they relate to your home. The idea is to determine whether you want to keep what you discover, or whether it's time to make some adjustments.

WHAT DO YOU SMELL?

Have you ever had guests stay the night and realized the next day that someone left behind a sweater, a scarf, or a jacket? When you pick up the item to put it in a closet or in your car to return it, have you noticed that it always has an odor? Every single time! The fabric holds a distinctive scent unique to its owner. You may have noticed the same smell on their other personal belongings or when entering their home.

Well, I hate to break it to you, but your belongings also have a lingering fragrance, and it all starts with the scents in your home. Mine too! The problem is that we can't really smell our own smell. You're working on identifying the major scents in your home through Yoga Nidra, but more often than not you've grown so accustomed to your home environment that you don't even realize the scents are there.

Think of walking into a fragranced body lotion store. It's overwhelming, yet the people working there get so used to it that they go about their day as if the potent fragrance cloud doesn't exist. This desensitizing of the ability to detect smells in your home environment is especially problematic if your home has a not-so-pleasant odor that you haven't detected. Unpleasant smells can come from a variety of things: mold, pets, frequently cooked foods, a specific type of laundry detergent, overly perfumed candles, or other fragrance-infused items.

Even if you do so subconsciously, one of the first things you notice when walking into someone's home is its scent. And we all know that first impressions are important. When someone walks into my home, my hope is that its scent is one of fresh flowers, clean laundry or newly mown grass (not to mention rainbows and birdsong!).

All too often, though, this isn't the case. You immediately know if your friends are fish lovers or frequently cook bacon. Such aromas linger in the air and permeate fabrics. You also recognize the homes that smell musty, like they need to be aired out, or the ones that have a slight odor of mold or mildew that has yet to be discovered.

I had a client who . . . moved into a home that had an overly sweet, perfumed smell. I'm sure the prior owner loved it, and maybe their guests enjoyed it too, but to my client it was nauseating. I couldn't find where the smell was coming from because it was everywhere! In order to remove the smell, we first painted the walls, and that helped, but not completely. With every drawer I opened, there it was again, even inside the closets. I was chasing this elusive fragrance that belonged to someone else. Finally, after scrubbing with detergent, sprinkling box after box of baking soda, and putting dry coffee grounds inside every drawer, it seemed to die down. Not until then did my client feel that her home was truly hers.

The only way to get completely real with yourself about the scent in your home is to have a candid friend come over and do a sniff test. Maybe even ask two or three friends independently. Brutal as this may sound, it really works. Also, the next time you return from a trip, breathe deeply as you step inside your door. It is important to understand what your home smells like, even if you can't smell it day to day. You want to walk in and have it smell (pleasantly) like *home*.

There are many ways to remove bad odors, and to change the fragrance of your home. My all-time favorite is to open the windows and doors every day to refresh the air. I now live in a sunny climate, so this is easy advice for me to hand out, I know. However, I was born and raised in Oregon. And not the sunny part of Oregon. We would go three months at a time without seeing much sun, but we sure saw our fair share of rain.

INSIDER'S TIP: On a daily basis, my mom opened all the windows and doors in our home for fifteen minutes to cleanse the air—in all kinds of weather. I hated it so much when I was younger that I can hardly believe I'm sharing this tip with you now, let alone that I've adopted this habit into my daily life. In the winter, my sister and I used to shiver as we watched the clock, continually asking, "Is it time yet?" The frigid air coming in didn't feel like a good trade-off for a freshened home back then, at least until the time was up, and then it was all worth it. But don't tell my mom I said that!

If you can get in the habit of airing out your home daily, the air you'll be breathing inside it will be so much healthier, and your home will smell better—naturally! It's my favorite way to breathe new life into my home. Both my husband and I have to travel a great deal for work, so I get that first scent impression more frequently than I like, as I'm often away for days on end. When I walk back in, I can always tell if the house has been shut up too tightly, or if, as I prefer, the doors have been left open so my dogs can come and go freely. The scent of my home gives it all away.

INSIDER'S TIP: Another favorite way to reduce odors naturally is to sprinkle baking soda on carpets, let it sit for an hour if you are able, but even fifteen minutes helps! Then vacuum it up. (This is something else I learned from my mom and have come to appreciate.) Baking soda absorbs and neutralizes odors, and it doesn't hurt your carpets or upholstered furniture. It's a snap to use, and it's economical, too.

While we're on the topic of baking soda, sprinkle it at the bottom of your trash can before inserting the bag, and try pouring a little down your sink drains with warm water, to keep them smelling fresh too.

Take a walk through your home. Open up every drawer and cabinet and look (and sniff) deep inside for any stuffy clothes, standing water from slow leaks, damp old boards, or hidden areas of the wall that might have mildew or mold. I recently discovered mildew under a client's kitchen sink cabinet. They had no idea it was there, and they had been opening that cabinet daily for cleaning supplies. Once we found the mildewed board, we had it cut out, then thoroughly dried the area and had a replacement board installed. Now their home smells so much better. Removing that one board made a huge difference.

Thinning out tightly grouped clothing in your closet and drawers can reduce odors by improving airflow. At the same time, identify any musty fabrics that might need to be rewashed.

Once you have addressed root causes of odors in your home, you can add fragranced candles, perfumes, and room sprays as desired. This way you're not masking odor, you're enhancing the fragrance of your clean home.

WHAT DO YOU HEAR?

Listen closely to the sounds in your home. Is what you hear pleasant? Is it calming? Or is it noise chaos, with the TV or radio blaring, dogs barking, and people talking—all at the same time. Add to that a fan with a loose blade or a buzz from a light fixture that needs to be fixed, and the effect can wreak havoc on your nerves.

Hopefully your home is frequently graced by music that you love, the happy sounds of an active family, and the natural sounds that you invite into your environment. Embrace those sounds.

Background noise from the TV or other ongoing sounds can be a constant source of subconscious agitation. Try eliminating as many of these noises as you can. Or at least invite them into your home on purpose, and, in the case of the TV, know that it's not on for the sake of being on. Make necessary repairs or replace light fixtures and other mechanical items no longer operating at their quiet best. Balance appliances and other items that vibrate when out of level. These, and other common household noises might seems like minor issues, but they can add up to major discomfort, ultimately eroding your quality of life.

Have you ever walked into an empty home and noticed that every footstep and voice sounds overly loud? If your home feels loud or even possibly echoey, try adding soft layers to create a more pleasing buffered tone. With each piece of upholstery, area rug, drapery, bedding, or throw that you invite into your home décor, you will simultaneously be absorbing and softening the sounds.

At first "the sound of silence" can be unnerving. But you don't have to go silent forever. Once you identify and suppress or remove annoying sounds, try gradually adding new, positive sounds—one by one—and see how it makes you feel. Only allow back in the sounds that make you smile.

Bring in a variety of sounds at specific times to set the tone, so to speak, or to help create the ambiance you want for a specific activity: festive music and the laughter of friends for a party, or soft music and a crackling fire for a cozy evening in. (Did you catch a hint of campfire smell? Your senses are powerfully connected! Something to remember.) Add a quietly burbling water fountain to accompany evening meditation. Or maybe you'll want to add joyful sounds to get your day started. Awaken to uplifting music or add an energetic soundtrack to keep you motivated during a morning exercise routine or dance session. Whatever the selected sound is, allow it in on purpose.

If you have road noise or something else beyond your control, try getting a white noise maker or something else that can mask the unpleasant noises that have become routine in your environment. Pay attention to the sounds in your home. Invite them in intentionally, and mask or eliminate any sounds that don't evoke a smile.

WHAT DO YOU FEEL AND TOUCH?

Our skin is the largest organ of our body. We have millions of tiny sensors (nerves) at work in our skin. To disregard the sense of touch in your home is to disregard the majority of your body. Looked at in this way, it seems silly to think the pleasure we take in our homes is perceived mostly through our sense of sight. We don't really pay enough attention to our sense of touch, do we? Or to any other sense, for that matter.

A scratchy tag on the back of your shirt can be a distraction the entire day. Even the residue from the stitching that is left partially behind when a tag is haphazardly ripped out can be a bother. What might sound like a tiny discomfort isn't tiny at all; it can disrupt your peace of mind. If it's not a tag that irritates you, maybe it's laundry soap residue. Or harsh airport hand soap. Or dust and dander that triggers allergies, rashes, and hives.

The fabrics and textures in your environment matter. Bring in the ones that welcome you home like a gentle embrace. Not everything has to be soft, but everything should be pleasurable to the touch.

Does the bedding you sleep on feel good against your skin? What do you feel under your feet, especially when you get out of bed? Is the floor shockingly cold and in need of a rug? Is the tile so hard it hurts your back or knees as you're doing the dishes? Add an anti-fatigue floor mat for comfort. Do you snag your clothes (and your skin) on the rough, splintered edges of the table where you eat most of your meals? Sand them smooth! Pay attention to the textures all around you. They should bring you pleasure and joy, or at a minimum, be subliminal textures that don't aggravate your nerves.

INSIDER'S TIP: There is a difference between ignoring textures and not noticing them. Take time to consider all the textures in your home at least once. Fix, get rid of, or replace the ones that are disturbing to your skin. You want to feel good in your home environment. Don't invite or allow irritating textures to linger in your home.

We have bedding, fabric, and towel samples all over our office. We're always in the midst of product development, which includes testing fabrics and weaving techniques from all over the world. It's hard to believe how completely different one bedsheet set can feel from another. You do have a choice when you bring textures and fabrics into your home. With as much variety as is on the market, there is no reason why you should buy or keep anything you don't enjoy, fabrics and textures included!

It amazes me that when my dogs come to my office, they always seek out the softest blanket or towel to claim as their bed for the day. Mind you, they are Labradoodles, one of the fluffiest dog breeds around. It's hard to even find their skin underneath all their fur. Jaxx, my oldest, will kick away pillows he doesn't like until he finds the one that is perfect for him. A dog! Yes, they're *my* dogs, so maybe they've acquired a sense for fabrics, but they're dogs nonetheless, and even they instinctively respond to fabrics that feel good to them. And, they have no guilt whatsoever about tossing aside what they don't like.

to care for. Ultimately, choose what feels the best to you and your family, whether or not it's on track with the latest trends.

Your sense of touch, how things feel, is important in your home environment. Just as you might not want to wear a scratchy wool sweater against your skin all day, you probably wouldn't choose to sit, sleep, or brush up against textures or fabrics that are irritating to you in your home. There are so many different textures and materials in this world, and that's for a reason. We're all different, and we each have unique preferences. Textures play a big part in the sensual enjoyment of your environment. As with anything, welcome into your home only what you love.

Temperature also plays an important role in how you *feel* in your home. You may have heard that 68 degrees is the most ideal for sleeping and 72°F is the perfect daytime temperature, but what matters the most is how each temperature affects the enjoyment of your environment. Determine your personal, or your family's personal comfort zone, and adjust it as you enter into different phases throughout the day.

While the exact temperature for ideal sleep is unable to be generalized, various studies indicate that adjusting the temperature of the room to between 60°F to 68°F can help you sleep longer and deeper. How many blankets and your normal body temperature will cause the ideal temperature of your bedroom to vary, so try to keep your bedroom cooler and experiment to see what *your* optimal temperature is.

When my husband sets our bedroom thermostat to 68°F I have to wear socks and sometimes even sweatpants to bed, removing layers as I warm up. However, if either of us wakes up in the middle of the night, reducing the temperature in the room helps us get back to sleep.

If you set the thermostat to 72°F during the day and the air feels stuffy, by all means turn the dial down. Determine the ideal temperature for you and your family in each area of your home, and try to keep it consistent within that space. It's a subtle thing, but it makes a difference in the overall enjoyment of your environment.

A NEW WAY OF LOOKING AT YOUR HOME

I want to let you in on a designer's secret, a whole new way of looking at your home.

When designers walk into a client's room, whether it be a home, a restaurant, or a hotel room, we try to take in the entire room at once. Unless there is an extremely bold statement in the room, designers see everything without picking apart any one element. We're viewing the room with "soft eyes" as an overview, getting the general impression. We either like it or we don't.

Oftentimes, when you, as a nondesigner, walk into your own home, you tend to look at the room with "intense eyes." You fixate on individual objects and details that you might love or hate, as opposed to taking in the entire room. You can't see the forest for the trees, so to speak. You focus on whether this goes with that, or the fact that you like this, or don't like that, and you lose perspective on how your home appears overall. You tend to get fixated on details when we look through intense eyes. In my own home, I catch myself doing this all the time!

Try softening your eyes when you walk into a room in your home. Literally, soften your gaze. Unclench your eye muscles. Relax your forehead and eyebrow muscles, your eyelids, your cheek muscles. You might not have even been aware until now, that you can clench your eyes, as you might your jaw or tongue. Soften your eyes and take in your whole room. Feel it, see it, and experience it. This will help you see what someone else does when they enter your home. Let your eyes dance through the whole room.

From this holistic perspective, with soft eyes, you can be more objective. You might have a beautiful room right in front of you and not have even known it! The flip side can also be true. Soft eyes can help you see the reality of the scale and balance of a room without fixating on one specific detail or element.

DOES PERSONAL TASTE REALLY AFFECT YOUR HOME?

Did you know that 65 to 72 percent of most people's daily calorie intake is consumed at home? A Nebraska University study by dietetics expert Martha J. Nepper proves that the food environment you create in your home can lead to weight loss, or gain, as well as affecting your overall well-being.[3] Taste—in the form of your personal style and organizational preferences—is very much part of your home, and whether you realize it or not, you have a home food environment.

How is your kitchen organized? Do you have healthy and fresh foods visible and accessible? Or are jars of candy and bags of chips the most visible and convenient foods to grab? Try setting up an environment that allows ready access to the food groups you want your family to enjoy regularly. Clear the cabinets of foods that are outdated or that make you feel guilty. (You know, the foods with which you are cheating on the healthy diet you really should stick to.) Throw the outdated food away, and put all the cheat foods into a bag to give away. We all need guilty-pleasure foods at times, but try to only bring in such treats for special occasions, and have a more discreet space or storage system for them.

When we get home from work or whatever else we've been busy with outside our home environment, it's easy to give in to impulse and grab things we don't really enjoy eating, or things that do us no good nutritionally and leave us feeling unsatisfied. (I've been caught behind the cabinet door with my hand in the chip bag many times, so I'm by no means a perfect role model here.) We probably wouldn't eat the way we do at home in front of strangers. Can you imagine sneaking Ho Hos behind the vending machine at work? Or eating your lunch over the sink in the break room? Sounds silly, right? Yet we do such things at home without thought of how they might be degrading our sensual appreciation of the food we eat and the home we eat it in.

What foods and flavors remind you of your current home? Or of the home you once shared with your mother, grandmother, or another person special to you? The sensation of taste and the memories we build around the dinner table are part of how we perceive our home. I'm not saying you need to be a gourmet cook or spend hours slaving over a stove preparing family heirloom recipes every night. But I do hope you consciously try to enjoy the eating process in your home as opposed to rushing through a meal, doing little better than shoving food in your mouth.

Whether you're alone or with friends and family, *where* you eat really does matter, and that's why most every home has a defined place for eating. Whether it be a spacious dining room, a small breakfast nook, or barstools pulled up to a kitchen counter, designating a comfortable spot to eat meals and snacks will help you be present and in the moment with every bite you take.

Setting up an area where you can enjoy the experience of eating is really quite simple. The first step is identifying appropriate dining location(s) in your home. The next step is creating the environment in that area to support the way you want to feel as you eat.

Fast food restaurants tend to have loud music and brightly colored walls, an environment designed to encourage you to eat large quantities, and quickly! While it can be wonderful to crank up some tunes and dance barefoot long into the night, when you sit down to eat a meal, soften the tone and set the volume to a gently calming level. Creating a tranquil environment around your eating area(s) will slow you down naturally. Invite sounds that soothe you as you dine. Doing so will help you be in the moment, so that you can savor your food and the company of those you have chosen to eat with.

To further support a calming experience, select wall colors that support the mood you want to create in the dining area. Paint walls in understated tones: variations of white, taupe, light gray, or understated pastels. Nothing too bold or jarring. When selecting your desired white, look for clues from other items in your room. Are your go-to colors warmer, like tans, reds, or golds? Then you would want a white with a warm undertone. If your furniture and fabrics are on the cooler side, with possibly a blue or gray hue, you would want to opt for a cooler white to complement the cool undertones—possibly a white that is subtly more gray. I get more into selecting paint colors a little later in the book.

Whether you are creating an eating space in the kitchen, dining room, family room, or home office, you need a surface on which to set down your plate. It should be at a height that feels comfortable to you. Although we have all eaten in front of the TV at times, to reduce mindless snacking while watching your favorite program, have a TV tray or mini side table that supports your plate. This gives you an intentional eating surface, and makes it much easier to balance your utensils so you can take a breath, and a pause, between bites, as opposed to shoveling it all in at once.

Feeling good about your eating experience and your food environment can be supported in other ways, too.

YOUR SIXTH SENSE: ENERGY AND INTUITION

I believe we all possess a sixth sense. Call it your gut feeling, your intuition, your knowing, or an instinctual feeling. Call it what you will, or don't identify it by name at all, but I think we can all agree that when we know something, we just know it. It's an energy from within or from beyond, depending on your spiritual beliefs.

When you walk into your home, or into a particular room, if it doesn't feel right, please don't ignore this feeling. Pay attention to it. Your best life has the potential to begin at home. It is the one environment you have the power to control and change, so tune in to what is going on *energetically* in your home.

How do you feel, in your core, about your home environment? If it's not right, you, and only you, possess the power to change it. You are powerful beyond what you might ever realize. Take action. Get rid of toxic elements and energies in your home. Only bring in things that feel good to your soul.

My family and I had few material possessions while I was growing up, so it was a big deal when my mom would spend what little money we had to buy something from a garage sale or Goodwill, as opposed to making it herself or receiving it as a hand-me-down from someone at our church. It therefore felt shocking to me when she would pile items in the middle of the living room floor, stating that there was something off about the energy they brought into our home, and that she was getting rid of them. I was thinking, *That's probably twenty bucks' worth of stuff! How can we just get rid of that? It's like throwing away real money!* Now I get it. Something about the items didn't feel right to her, and she didn't want them in our home. Pay attention to what you bring into your home. Do you love it? Does it bring you joy? If not, no matter what you paid for it, get rid of it.

Treat your home like the sanctuary it should be. Only invite in positive energy that will allow you and your family to flourish.

You are always hearing, seeing, smelling, feeling, and tasting. When you set up your home environment, take all of these into account.

You experience the world through all of your senses. They are alive and alert at all times, even though we frequently take them for granted. You are always hearing, seeing, smelling, feeling, and tasting. When you set up your home environment, take all of these into account.

One way to get present and really know what elements in your home affect your nonvisual senses is to try the Yoga Nidra exercise. By focusing on each of your senses, try to experience your home as if it were for the first time. Be aware of what you smell, hear, touch, taste, and see. Through your senses, evaluate your possessions as well as the less tangible smells, sounds, and tastes.

Then consider: would you intentionally invite these elements you are experiencing into your home? Or not? Do they support the environment you desire for your well-being and happiness? If they don't, get rid of them, or if they can be fixed, fix them. Plain and simple.

Action Item

PAYING ATTENTION THROUGH ALL OF YOUR SENSES

- Pay as much attention to the nonvisual elements that make up your home as you do to the elements you can see.

- Be present with each of your six senses.

- Be aware of what exists in your home.

- If you don't like what you experience, fix it or change it.

- Identify and clear out odors.

- Fix or replace uncomfortable textures.

- Allow in sounds intentionally, mask or eliminate the rest.

- Set up your home food environment in a way that supports well-being.

- Only welcome things into your home that energetically support the environment you want to create for yourself and your family.

PART II

Getting Started

3

What's Holding
You Back?

*Inaction breeds doubt and fear. Action breeds confidence
and courage. If you want to conquer fear, do not sit at home.
Go out and get busy!*

Dale Carnegie

Why aren't you living in a home that sets you up for your best life *now*? Many of us put off making our home an environment in which we can thrive, because of "holdbacks" such as a fear of change, feelings of inadequacy or insecurity, or worries that we're not creative enough to pull it off. Sometimes we put off improving our home out of guilt for wanting more; you feel you should be content with what you have. Another big holdback is feeling that you are not as deserving as others.

We self-sabotage our potential to live in a house that **delights** us, a place we would love coming home to, without **even** realizing we're doing it.

Most often these limiting feelings are subconscious. We self-sabotage our potential to live in a house that delights us, a place we would love coming home to, without even realizing we're doing it. Even though I know better now, I used to slip into patterns of feeling unworthy or insecure. We all have some version of these vulnerable feelings. Left unchecked, they can block you from creating a healthy, happy, beautiful, and well-functioning home environment that suits your individuality and the way you truly want to live. It's important to learn how to identify these self-destructive feelings, and move beyond the negativity before it takes hold.

We can mask our own feelings with excuses, which can cause paralysis. Frequently we think we'll wait to do anything until we have more time, more money. Or until we get our *next* home. We tell ourselves that our *next* home will be the right home, and *that's* the right time to really start thinking about an environment to support our best life. Some folks settle into the status quo for years, even if it's less than ideal, thinking, *It's not in the cards at this time.* "At this time" can become "never" if you let it!

Coming from humble beginnings, my subconscious used to suggest that nice homes were for everyone else. Not for me. So my natural tendency used to be that with every step-up house, I would pile guilt on myself. I finally realized that I am really the only one who can change—no one else is going to wave a magic wand and take away my feelings of unworthiness. Through substantial study, experience, and observation, I've learned that it's easy to self-sabotage

our greatest dreams. I've also come to understand that self-realization—taking complete ownership of and responsibility for our choices, actions, and thought patterns—is the only way to move beyond self-imposed limitations. It has taken significant work on my part to get to this point of being able to fully embrace *my home*. My home, and my husband's too, that we both worked hard to create.

Whatever you might be battling, whatever is standing in the way of having a home that supports your best life—not enough money, fear of failure, feelings of unworthiness, lack of time, and so on—believe me, I've been there. I can relate all too well. That is exactly why I know I can help you out of your limiting habits and patterns, and help you rise to extraordinary heights in your own home. Home is where it all begins.

Let's explore a little more deeply a few of the most common limiting behaviors. You can decide whether you identify with any of them, and if so, how closely. Identification is the first step. Taking complete personal responsibility to rise above the patterns and holdbacks is the second step. Once you do this, you can nip those holdbacks in the bud, and move on!

REDESIGNING MY HOME COSTS TOO MUCH...IT WILL CAUSE ME TO GO BROKE...

The idea of redesigning one's home is a nonstarter for many, since they think it will be prohibitively expensive. This is a common stumbling block; in fact, it's the one I see most often. It's why so many homes are chaotic and disheveled, in a state of "maybe someday" or surrounded by half-finished projects. This negative-energy state can actually prevent opportunities from flowing into your life, since you don't have a grounding home base established to support all your endeavors and goals. Letting financial fears hold you back can leave you feeling frustrated, discontented, and wishing for something better in your home but never actually turning your desires into actionable steps.

Your home should be your personal sanctuary, a place that evokes feelings of tranquility and provides respite from the busy world around you.

Your home is also a major investment in your quality of life. The good news is that creating an environment in which you can thrive doesn't *have* to cost a lot of money at all.

Resourcefulness helps! Remember my story of changing the color of my shag carpet? I know what's it like to have zero dollars—in my case, zero nickels—to spend on a home. I'll be sharing tips that don't cost money, as well as many that may stretch you a bit. But that's where my budgeting tips and step-by-step planning will come into play. Like the planning needed to achieve any dream or goal in life, you have to start somewhere. You can begin your journey of readying your home today—empty pockets or not!

Setting intentions doesn't cost any money at all but makes a big impact.

Your home environment is deeply affected by setting your intentions, a basic step that is often overlooked when facing an avalanche of choices related to the best furniture, the trendiest colors, or the latest technology. Setting intentions doesn't cost any money at all but makes a big impact. Of course there are decisions to be made about the aspects of design, organization, function, placement, and color choice, and I'll get into all of these with more detail later, but for now I want to assure you that you can work with your existing possessions if you wish. You don't need to buy a new sofa in order to have one in the right color or in the right place.

Whether you will make some big purchases along the way or not, over the course of this book I'll show you how to use a Vision Board to identify how you want your dream home to look and feel. With this in mind, any purchases you make or projects you take on today will fit into your overall vision of your dream home. Starting with a Vision Board releases the fear that you're burning money on something, only to have to replace it or redo it later when you have more money to spend, or move to a different house. It helps you feel assured that any money you spend now is a worthwhile investment in the future.

By the time you finish this book, you will have all the tools to know what works and what doesn't in your home environment, not only from a design standpoint but also in regard to what suits your unique style. Together, we'll be expanding your thought process to really tap into what it is you want in your home.

I'll share everything I know, but don't worry, there won't be any boxes of dye in your future. At least not for your carpet, as I won't make you go through the same design experiments I did along the way. However, you will learn some valuable, low-cost or no-cost ways to make your *now* home a version of your *dream* home.

I DON'T DESERVE IT ...
I FEEL GUILTY ...

One of my dear friends recently moved into a beautiful new home that she and her family built from the ground up. She had grown up in a low-income household, faced with many extremely challenging life circumstances. Despite all of this, she'd forged ahead to create a better life for herself and her children. She worked incredibly hard for every single penny that it took to build this house.

The weekend she finally got to move in to her new home, she called me and said, "I don't know what we were thinking! This place is big, we don't need it. I'm just a wreck! We're going to sell it!" Then it hit me that she wasn't comfortable because she didn't feel she deserved this in her life. This beautiful home that she and her husband had worked so hard to dream up, save for, and build was an uneasy new reality for her. As an outside observer, it was so obvious that she, of all people, deserved this home. But no matter how great living in this new house might appear to others, she couldn't identify with her new reality.

Feelings of inadequacy or guilt, of being undeserving, can hold you back in life, whether in business, in your personal life, or in your home environment—the place you start and end your day. You are every bit as deserving of a well-functioning home as anyone else. You weren't born less deserving than the president of the United States or any celebrity you see on TV.

I used to carry around the baggage, or limiting behavior, of feeling undeserving like it was a disease I was born with. I was always so happy for everyone else who had a home that "just felt right." In fact, I loved doing the design work for them. Yet subconsciously I never felt deserving of it for myself. Early in my journey, anytime I would move in to a home that was a step up, a little bit nicer, I abruptly wanted to put it up for sale or move.

Whenever I would move, my home was not a priority for me, but everyone else's home was. I'd help a friend pick out a paint color or reorganize, while my home was still in boxes and not pulled together. As a teenager, I spent years cleaning people's homes to give them a clean, organized, tidy environment, and then I spent more years designing beautiful, well-functioning homes for everyone except me. At that point I was still thinking, *Who am I to be deserving of a wonderful home of my own?*

It wasn't until I identified this as a major challenge that I had to overcome, that I was able to embrace my home. My HOME. Not just a house that gave me shelter.

I realized this was a pattern that held me back in several areas in my life. Once, I was on a trip to Hawaii with my husband. We both work hard, yet I felt guilty for being on vacation. Though it was only a five-day trip, I couldn't help sneaking in a little work each day. I told my husband not to post any photos on social media; I felt selfish and undeserving.

Fortunately, my husband doesn't battle with the same limiting behaviors and feelings. Any thought of that nature is absolutely foreign and ridiculous to him. He looked at me and said, "Well, then this trip is being wasted on you. You might as well not be here." That comment stopped me in my tracks. My first thought was, *That's unfair*, but that twinge of truth struck me to my core. He was right! Our trip was completely wasted on me, because I was lost in my feelings of guilt as opposed to being in the moment. In Hawaii! Enjoying the sunset, breathing in the fresh air. Really embracing the gift I had been given.

Choosing gratitude rather than guilt has changed my world. It has lent an entirely new reality to everything I experience in life.

I now carry that lesson through every aspect of my life. Once I identified that self-sabotaging problem, I was able to shake it, and now I catch myself before I allow it to take hold and ruin a wonderful situation. Like thriving in my beautiful home. When I go to gratitude, my entire reality instantly changes. Choosing gratitude rather than guilt has changed my world. It has lent an entirely new reality to everything I experience in life. That awakening has helped me be in the present moment and feel deserving. This has taken serious practice on my part, and though I've gotten better, I continue to work on this holdback.

INSIDER'S TIP: One of my favorite books that touches on this topic of limiting beliefs and behaviors is *The Power of Now* by Eckhart Tolle:

"As soon as you honor the present moment, all unhappiness and struggle dissolve, and life begins to flow with joy and ease. When you act out of the present-moment awareness, whatever you do becomes imbued with a sense of quality, care, and love—even the most simple action."[4]

Tolle also says (and I agree),"Gratitude for the present moment and the fullness of life is true prosperity."[5]

Now when I'm in a great environment or having an amazing experience—enjoying a delicious dinner, touring a beautiful city, or even having a free afternoon to sit in my backyard with a glass of wine—instead of feeling guilty, I feel grateful. It takes a conscious shift in mind-set. When I go to gratitude, my entire reality instantly changes, positively affecting everything I experience in life.

INSIDER'S TIP: *The Magic*, by Rhonda Byrne, has such great reminders about gratitude. One of my favorites is, "When you wake up to the new day today, before you move, before you do a single thing, say the magic words, thank you." She goes on to say,

"Your life is a gift, every day is a gift, and when you really think about it, it's inconceivable that any of us would wake up in the morning without giving thanks for another day. If you think a new day isn't such a big deal, then just try missing one!"[6]

You deserve a home where you can flourish, as much as anyone else does. Oftentimes we diminish ourselves while we build up others. This plays out in our homes, too. Once you identify this pattern in your behavior, it's amazing what doors will open up for you. This includes your ability to create a home that is perfectly suited for you.

I'M NOT THE CREATIVE TYPE...

Is *I'm not the creative type* your go-to excuse? If so, I hate to break it to you, but you are! Everyone is creative; you need to trust yourself and tap into your creativity. And I'm going to show you how.

The creative part of a person's brain is like a muscle; if it gets used, it will become stronger.

Some say our brains are capable of science, math, art, language, creativity, music, and space:

"Creativity does not involve a single brain region or single side of the brain. Instead, the entire creative process—from preparation to incubation to illumination to verification—consists of many interacting cognitive processes (both conscious and unconscious) and emotions. Depending on the stage of the creative process, and what you're actually attempting to create, different brain regions are recruited to handle the task."[7]

So there is no way you can say you weren't born with the creative side of your brain. Creativity comes from all parts of your brain, and it is like a muscle; if it gets used, it will become stronger.

As a designer and writer, I'm constantly trying to stimulate my creativity. If you haven't tapped into that creative part of yourself in awhile, it just takes a few tools, some practice, and some effort on your part. Designers work at it all the time. They learn to use whatever gifts they have and be creative with the rest. Anybody can do this, starting at any time. Here are a few of my favorite tools to spark creativity.

- **Record it.** Keep a notebook or a camera (or both) with you to record your thoughts, ideas, and inspirations. My phone has a memo app that I use like a notebook. Sometimes I even write a little note on a piece of paper and take a picture of that! Whatever works for you. The key is to start keeping track of things you like and find interesting, even if you don't know why you like them. Eventually you'll organize your notes and use these photos on your Vision Board, but for now, look and record. And remember, if you start looking for inspiration, you'll find it quicker.

- **Start your education.** Go shopping! Eventually you'll be buying pieces for your home. With education comes confidence, and, shopping can be informative. But don't buy anything yet. Ask questions, sit on sofas, touch fabrics, take pictures. Look at prices. This will give you a feel for quality and a sense of who's selling the styles you like. Grab their catalog, cut out your favorite images, and save them for your Vision Board. For right now, don't limit yourself by your budget, either. Shop in the high-end stores and boutiques; what the heck, browsing is free! Visit thrift stores, estate sales, outlets, and discounters too. I also love to visit craft shops, artist studios, and handmade furniture workshops, especially when I travel.

- **Discover the power of observation.** One of the aspects that greatly impacts my creativity is by staying curious and present in my environment. I enjoy watching the world around me. I'm observant and inquisitive, and I've been that way forever.

According to a study on this subject, "people with robust observation skills, whether inherent or learned through extensive training, showed superior creativity levels compared to other participants."[8] You too can improve your observation skills, thus becoming more creative, simply by being mindful about your environment. Pay attention. We miss a lot of the world by shuffling from here to there, and the best part of this, is it is completely under your control to be present and mindful of your environment. You can train yourself to pay attention again. Wherever you are, be there![9]

Action Item

WHAT TO DO WHEN YOU ARE STUCK OR IN A CREATIVE SLUMP

No matter what your day job is, we all get to that point when new thoughts aren't happening, and we have lost our creative edge. Call it writer's block, being fresh out of ideas, or being tired, stressed, and overwhelmed by options. Whatever you call it, it's not a fun feeling. You're stuck. So go do something else. Go outside—observe and feel the natural beauty around you. Or take yourself on a date with art—visit a museum, a bookstore, or an art gallery. Try something new and different.

To jump-start my brain or reinspire myself, I often meditate. At first the concept of quieting my brain in order to break out of a creative slump puzzled me. Why would I waste time and energy thinking of nothing when I could be putting my brain to work? Now when I'm feeling stuck, a few minutes in meditation does the opposite of what I originally thought. Giving my brain permission to just be reignites my creativity, and I usually come out of meditation with my brightest ideas to address my biggest challenges.

Another great way to reinspire yourself is to get moving. Going for a walk, doing yoga—anything—fires up my creativity. When I'm doing any of these activities I try to look at everything I see with wonderment. Really be in the moment. It's amazing how this sparks my imagination!

IT WILL RUIN MY MARRIAGE, PARTNERSHIP, RELATIONSHIPS...

Have you overheard your friends arguing over their decorating or renovation project? Possibly one of them has even spent the night on your sofa! Or have you yourself gotten knee-deep into a project before realizing that you and your partner are fighting about it constantly and can't seem to find common ground? The arguments are typically about things that are so minor you might not even remember what triggered the emotions in the first place.

For some, the fear that designing a home will hurt a relationship is real, so if it's your holdback, know that you're not alone. You might be thinking, why rock the boat? This is common when embarking on a new home project together. However, it doesn't mean the project is wrong and that you should avoid it all together, or that you are with the wrong partner.

Being unique individuals—different from each other—doesn't mean you can't create a home environment where everyone thrives together. In fact, this is when it's the most critical.

Whether you're married, roommates, or with a new partner and sharing a place for the first time, you and the person you are living with may have come from diverse backgrounds and had a multitude of different life experiences up until this point. It's no wonder you have different opinions, style tastes, and sets of priorities. Being unique individuals—different from each other—doesn't mean you can't create a home environment where everyone thrives together.

To help you to a point of shared vision and common goals, you can implement some ground rules early on and take advantage of some tools we'll discuss more deeply in chapter 5. It's all about communication, respect, collaboration, and compromise, and your Vision Board will play a key role, You are most definitely capable of pulling this off!

I DON'T OWN MY DREAM HOME NOW . . . I SHOULD WAIT . . .

There is no reason to put off getting your *now* home set up to support your best life, even if it's for a short time. Thinking you should wait to get started until after you have your dream home is almost as common as thinking that redesigning your home will cost too much and cause you to go broke. These are both excuses for not moving forward toward living your best life.

For a variety of reasons, more and more people are choosing not to buy a house at all. Others are choosing to move around more often to enjoy exploring a variety of living circumstances and locations. If this is you, it's perfectly fine (and probably tons of fun), but there is no reason to live in an unorganized environment that isn't fulfilling your needs and desires—especially not out of boxes!

Home ownership does not magically give someone the right to live a better life at home.

Home ownership does not magically give someone the right to live a better life at home. Rented and shared houses are homes, and can and should be set up to support the best living environment for everyone living there now. All of the same principles apply to rented homes as to homes that are purchased. Even if you rent one room in a home, the same design and organizational principles apply to your rented bedroom that would apply to a bedroom in a home that you owned.

No matter if where you currently live is short term or long term, you can still set an intention for *how* you want to live that will greatly affect your life now. You can still set up a Vision Board to expand your vision for how you want your home, or your room, to look and feel. You can still put together a Project List for organizing, decorating, and purchasing.

Are you worried that what you purchase now might not work in your next home? Then it's even more important that you take the first two steps mentioned above: setting an intention and creating a Vision Board before you purchase anything. This will ensure that you have expanded your long-range vision and know that the look and feel you want will be lasting and will transition well—without limiting yourself to your current circumstances.

INSIDER'S TIP: If you do intend to move soon, try to purchase only those items that you love, and in common sizes. If you are in a temporary home, this may not be the time to purchase a tiny dining room table that won't expand, or a massive two-piece sectional that can only be put together in one way. However, if you want a sectional, and you know you'll be moving soon, you could opt to purchase a modular style that comes in several pieces to allow you to expand or decrease its size. Also, for larger-sized pieces like sofas, consider opting for classic neutral tones that will help them blend into your next home. With these neutrals as a basis, it's a snap to change out accent items, such as decorative pillows and area rugs, as your tastes evolve.

One thing that is constant in life is change. If I had a dollar for all the clients who told me that they were designing for their last and final home, only to sell it within the following two years, I might have been able to retire years ago. Knowing you will have an eventual move is an advantage: you get to be more mindful in your decision-making process, selecting items that will transition smoothly and are exactly in line with the vision you have on your boards. The prospect of moving should not be an excuse to put off improving your home now.

I had a client who . . . was a professional athlete. Living that life, moving was pretty much inevitable. In fact, he and his family had already relocated three times over the past several years. They were now positioned in a new state, with a new home, a new set of schools for their kids, and the task of once again making all new friends. When I asked them if they were tired of "starting over" and so frequently, they acknowledged that it does get tiring but that the trade-off of setting up their home each time, and not living out of boxes, was worth it no matter how long they got to live in their *now* home. Whenever they put off making their home an environment that really suited their family and the way they wanted to live, everything suffered—from his performance on the court to the kids' in school.

I DON'T HAVE THE RIGHT SKILLS...

You may not have all the skills you wish you had, but you will learn from your mistakes! With some basic instruction and tips, you will be able to take on a number of DIY design projects and home improvements. But know some projects really are best left to licensed professionals. Trust me on this. Hire out any work related to electricity, plumbing, water, or your walls, roof, and floor, or that require heavy equipment or tall ladders. Stick to projects you can transition to your next house, or tasks that don't require making permanent changes. Try a new task with the help of a friend who has done it before, and read as much as you can about the project before you begin. If it doesn't work out, you can change it or redo it later.

I DON'T HAVE ENOUGH TIME...

Be resourceful and keep your projects small when your time is at a premium. Break larger projects into smaller tasks you can finish in an evening or a weekend. And later in the book, I'll share with you some effective tips and ideas that will help organize your time. You will feel so proud knowing you accomplished a task you never thought possible, even if it's a small one!

I CAN'T IDENTIFY MY STYLE OR FIGURE OUT WHAT I REALLY WANT...

Your style will evolve over time, so don't worry that you might not have it nailed down right now. Many of my clients who thought they could identify their style on our first meeting, later realized that their true style was far different than they thought. What helped them figure it out? Visualization tools. Your Vision Board will help identify what you like, as well as what you don't like. It will help you assemble well-balanced and harmonious rooms, and even position each item in or around the room.

Own It!

What is holding *you* back? Consider a project you want to do or have already started. What prevents you from moving forward? Be honest with yourself, and dig deep. Only you have the power to change self-limiting behaviors. And you are powerful enough to overcome any of these obstacles.

Feelings of fear, guilt, insecurity, or of being undeserving are all normal. I've found that even my most successful clients have insecurities around making decisions for their homes. No matter where you are in your stage of life, know that once you recognize your self-limiting thoughts and behaviors, it'll be easier to accept them and take responsibility for your actions, or lack thereof. It takes practice to keep moving forward with a project even if you recognize your holdbacks.

Action Item

IDENTIFYING HOLDBACKS AND TAKING RESPONSIBILITY

- Identify any feeling or obstacle, internal or external, that might be holding you back from making changes or working toward your dream home in your *now* home.

- List tasks or projects you've started around your home but haven't completed, or that you want to do but have never started.

- What are the reasons (excuses?) that you never finished these tasks? Be thorough, and be honest!

- Are there deeper behaviors behind your holdbacks? List them. These are your limiting behaviors.

- Write down three or more ways you can take personal responsibility to overcome each of your limiting behaviors.

4

The Magic of a Vision Board

See the world not as it is, but what it could be,
if only you believe in courage, and kindness, and
occasionally, just a little bit . . . of magic.

Fairy Godmother, Cinderella, 2015

We all need a little bit of magic in our lives, and Visions Boards are just that for me. I use them for everything, especially my biggest, most important goals and dreams in life. They have helped make even my most outrageous dreams come true. I could tell you example after example, but that's for my next book! For now, I'll keep the examples geared toward how you can use Vision Boards to create your dream environment in your *now* home.

Your home is where everything in your life begins, and making it better is not something to put off for someday. Applying Vision Board techniques to your home environment makes it simpler to achieve the desired result you want in your home right now. Your home environment is a springboard for all other areas in your life. It is incredibly powerful, and deserving of your attention now.

Visualization gives you the power to see things how you truly want them to be.

Visualization is a tool for setting goals and actualizing results and experiences. Vision Boards are one of the tools used in visualization. Visualization gives you the power to see things how you truly want them to be. This tool has been used for centuries, though some people still relegate it to the vague realm of free spirits, hippies, and dreamers.

Now in the mainstream, visualization is practiced by people from all parts of the world and all walks of life to envision success through mental imagery. Athletes and coaches often use visualization techniques to practice skills and see each shot, effort, or play before their event. It helps them picture a desired outcome, a successful result—every time. And you can use these same techniques when it comes to getting the home environment you want and deserve.

HOW A VISION BOARD WORKS

I will first walk you through an overview of what a Vision Board is and how it works. At the end of the chapter, under the Action Items, you will find my step-by-step process for creating one.

GETTING STARTED

Your personal Vision Board can be a framed corkboard or a fabric-covered bulletin board hanging on your wall, a white poster board you lean anywhere, or even a cardboard shoebox so no one else but you sees your images. My first Vision Board was a three-ring binder. I used clear pocket pages along with tabs for the various topics. You can also use apps on your phone. Pinterest acts as a good backdrop for a Vision Board. Use whatever method is most convenient for you and allows you to conveniently see it every day. If it's something that takes a few clicks to get to, I recommend setting a reminder alert on your phone to open up the app and take a peek at least once a day. Engaging with your Vision Board daily is key, whether it's adding to it or just looking at it for a few minutes. Out of sight can become out of mind. And you want your dreams at the top of your mind. Always.

Once a framed corkboard or poster board is working well for me, it's something I want to display, so I can see it every day, numerous times, without even trying. At first, I was too embarrassed to let others see my Vision Board. I felt vulnerable. It was like whoever saw my Vision Board was peeking into my soul. When I had guests, I would move my board into my closet. Now that I've been doing this for years and credit my Vision Board for many of my dreams coming true, I've gained the confidence to proudly display it in my office or at home for everyone to see, all day long. Ultimately, where you place your Vision Board and with whom you share it is completely up to you.

For the purposes of this book, your goal is to create a specific Dream Home Vision Board, which will be loaded with images and phrases pertaining only to your dream home. Seeing the inspiring images and written phrases and affirmations of what you want to experience in your home—the feelings and the aesthetics—can help make these things come true.

Tried and True Designer Tool

Designers have been using this process of image boards for decades. I have used Vision Boards for my life goals, and put together image boards or Project Inspiration Boards for clients. Once while I was creating a Project Inspiration Board for a particular client, it hit me that I was actually creating the very same thing as a Vision Board, but for their house!

These Project Inspiration Boards are a gathering of images that exemplify various trends, colors, styles, and emotions to help clients define their taste and style. Designers have more options available to us than the general public does, so this is how we expand our clients' vision, helping them avoid feeling restricted to what they may have seen before. We create these boards with lots of images at first, and then, with the client, we weed out what they don't like, over and over again, before we get into anything specific pertaining to their final home purchases or material selections. This ensures that our client will love exactly what we come up with for them.

We expand and exemplify their vision to confirm that we're on track before we start in on the design project. We would NEVER just go out and start shopping. Never. That would result in unhappy clients and time wasted running around returning things. We even have a flowchart of how we make the decisions and the purchases. You'll be learning all of that, so you can do this process too! For now, just dream. And dream big. This vital first step is shaping your dream home, *now* and in the *future*.

COLLECTING IMAGES AND PHRASES

To gather images for your Vision Board, tear out photos, quotes, song lyrics, prayers, mantras, meaningful words and phrases from magazines and brochures, (if you see an inspiring image in a book, take a photo and print it) the old fashioned way, which I still do all the time. You can also use the internet to find almost anything you want. Search, print, and pin them to the board (or pin to your Pinterest). It's a breeze! It's even better than online shopping because you can pick whatever image you want. Even the most expensive ones!

It's also fun to drive around and take photos with your phone, then either post or print and pin them to your Vision Board. The more images and phrases you collect, the better your dream home will evolve. And noting what you don't like is equally as helpful to identifying what you do like.

As you get started, remember to gather images and text related to how you want to feel, and to experiences you want to have in your home. These are as important as the visual look itself. For example, you might want to create the home experience of being unencumbered and flexible to travel, so you want to find images and phrases that reflect and support this lifestyle. All of this matters.

If you're not sure about an image, save it anyway. Choose whatever interests you for whatever reason, even if you don't know why you like the image. Don't limit yourself in any way when gathering your images. The more the better to start. You can edit later. Now is the time to dream big.

INSIDER'S TIP: Don't worry if the photos you choose are considered current, on-trend, or not. All trends evolve. You can make anything work from a design standpoint. We'll get into all of that a little later on—making things work and come together isn't magic that is only granted to designers. You'll soon have the most important fundamental tools to pull it off. However, this first step toward creating your Dream Home Vision Board is to simply collect your dream images and whatever is interesting to you.

EXPANDING YOUR VISION

For your first Dream Home Vision Board, disregard your *now* home completely. Free your mind of any restrictions. If all you had was pure potential to live anywhere you wanted, where would you choose? No financial constraints, no outside influences from family, friends, neighbors, coworkers, or colleagues; you can live anywhere in the world and experience any weather or lifestyle. What do *you* want? Where would you live? Would you have a two-story home, or one? Or three? Is your home open and free-flowing, or more traditional with individual, designated gathering rooms? What colors appeal to you? What pieces of furniture jump out at you? What emotions do you want to feel in your home? Excitement and fun, or tranquility and calm? Remember all of it is good! What matters most is that it's exactly what you want it to be.

For many, this journey of dreaming big brings about feelings of inadequacy and unworthiness. Remember, as we discussed in the last chapter, these limiting feelings are holdbacks for almost everything in life. Not dreaming big enough is the root of much mediocrity and unhappiness. Dig deep and release limiting beliefs and behaviors about yourself and your circumstances. Take the time to be present and identify what it is you truly want in your life and in your home. Only when you do these things can you ultimately create a home that is uniquely suited for you and your family. The first step is to expand your vision and get clear on what you want and need. Trust yourself, free yourself. Give yourself permission to dream as big as you possibly can during this stage of your design process!

Gather as many images as you can, because as you start to pin them to the board, you'll realize that you like some images more than others. As you remove any image, I recommend saving them in a folder so you can come back to them if needed. For some reason, it's hard to completely throw away an image and this is a great way to edit without dealing with getting rid of something permanently. Plus, you may change your mind later.

There's no right or wrong way to do this. Actually, there is a wrong way—dreaming too small.

Collecting and editing images is a fun and inspiring process. Each person in your family can join in and create their own board, or you can do one board together. It can be a family Dream Home Vision Board, one that everyone contributes to. There's no right or wrong way to do this. Actually, there is a wrong way—dreaming too small. Vision Boards are meant to expand your vision. Dream as big as you can. Bigger! What would you do if you knew you could not fail? You can have anything you want, so what do you truly want? Choose your images with that thought in mind.

When you put your images on your board, they should be semifixed, as opposed to glued in place. I use tacks or pins for a cork or bulletin board, magnets for a metal surface, or repositionable tape for a white board, foam core, or cardboard. Creating a Vision Board is a journey, and you don't want to be too strict or rigid with your selections. You can substitute the images for new ones anytime and move them all around again and again.

INSIDER'S TIP: If you remove images related to a dream that came true, save them in a separate folder. It is so much fun to look back on these images, and it helps pick you up when you feel over-whelmed or a little hopeless, when your confidence in your own ability sinks. As in our day-to-day lives, we all go through highs and lows in the process of putting our home together. Reminding ourselves that we've already pulled off dreams, goals, hopes, and aspirations, is a reaffirming way to give your confidence a boost, and feel excited and positive again.

Law of Attraction

Besides identifying what your dream home looks and feels like, a Vision Board also has a certain type of manifesting magic to it. It works with the law of attraction, which suggests that positive outcomes will come from positive thinking. My all-time-favorite book, *The Secret*, by Rhonda Byrne, demonstrates this theory and has been used by tens of millions people around the globe.

A Vision Board has the power to attract and manifest whatever you want, in some sense—a home and an environment you probably never thought you could afford. A home that you would have always thought was destined for someone else, not you! Vision boards work with the law of attraction. By putting out what you want into the universe, and into your mind, you attract more of what you want in your life. The law of attraction is a very real, and very powerful thing.

MAGIC AT WORK

The most amazing thing happened to me a few years ago. It caught me completely off guard, and to me proves the power of Vision Boards. Not that I was a doubter to begin with.

My husband and I bought a home in my dream city, San Diego, the city that I had on my Vision Board for years. By this point, I had already launched my product-development business and was taking fewer and fewer design clients, as I simply didn't have the time. So all the design books I used for years for client inspiration had long been packed away. I was finally living my personal business dream—creating home furnishing products and design content to reach out to and help a multitude of people, instead of designing for one person or family at a time.

As I was unpacking in San Diego, I ran across a hardcover book that was missing its front cover. It was tattered and worn from use. Pages heavily tabbed. It was a design book my design team and I used to develop Project Inspiration Boards for several clients. Back then, we thumbed through coffee-table books and magazines to find the images we wanted to show a client. Because coffee-table books were expensive, when we found images that worked we would reuse the images frequently to show to other clients. We didn't want to

destroy the original book, so we would copy the images that we needed. Now we have the luxury of using Google, Pinterest, and Houzz to find images, which makes the process so much faster.

Naturally most designers have a particular style and lean toward personal preferences when selecting images. It's really tough to recommend an aesthetic you don't personally admire on some level.

I thumbed through the worn-out book, reminiscing. I turned to a page that had several tabs on it . . . and there was my home! Seriously. The home I was sitting in at that very moment was staring me in the face from my own open design book. The same home I had pinned on many clients' project boards over the past several years. I wouldn't believe it if it hadn't happened to me! I was dumbstruck!

What was even more amazing is that it wasn't just the house itself, it was also the furnishings that were included in the purchase price when we bought it. The photos in the book contained the same furnishings that were in my home right at that moment. It was a model home built ten years earlier. It was still exactly the same. Same accessories on the shelves, in exactly the same spots, down to the same patio furniture. None of it had changed since it had been photographed for the book.

All this time, I had no reminiscence that I had ever seen this home before I viewed it with a real estate agent. And there I was, unpacking my boxes in the very home that I had pinned images of, on vision/project boards many times for other people . . . and now it was mine. Unbelievable! But true.

So I'm telling you, Vision Boards have power. Use them and expect the unexpected to happen. The law of attraction in full force.

INSIDER'S TIP: When you're creating the first Vision Board for your home, dream big. Dream SO big, as more will come true than you could ever have believed to be possible. And choose your images carefully, as those images may truly become your home!

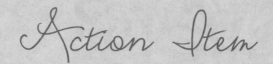

Action Item

CREATING YOUR DREAM HOME
VISION BOARD

- Create a Dream Home Vision Board that reflects the definition of your personal, most fulfilling dream home.

- Select what format you'll use to create your Vision Board—whatever works best for you.

- Gather lots of images and phrases that inspire you.

- Place the ones you love the most on a board.

- When your board is complete, put it somewhere you can see daily.

- Add and subtract new images as you find them or as inspiration hits, as often as you want.

How is your Dream Home Vision Board coming along? Don't feel like you have to finish your board, it's always going to be a work in progress. Vision Boards aren't ever 100 percent completed; they'll be done enough for now, done enough for you to get started on your real home. You can always add and change it as you move forward. And, you will! I can hear you thinking, so all this dreaming is great, but how does it help me today? How does it apply to my situation right now? Well, that's what the entire rest of this chapter is all about! This step is about using your Dream Home Vision Board to figure out your personal style.

Now that you have your Vision Board well under way, look at it overall for recurring themes. The key is to see the board as a whole, but also to notice the elements in each image. You might identify similar color tones, similar styles. Heavily patterned fabrics? Or no pattern at all? Possibly you'll discover that you prefer solid fabrics.

You might also notice that there are a number of nuances, like trees and plants versus no greenery, or area rugs versus no area rugs. You probably selected your images with only big goals in mind, like I asked you to do, but you'll soon learn much more by studying these images in different ways:

- Do you see an abundance of accessories or do most of the photos show rooms that are minimal?

- Art on the walls or no art at all?

- Light-colored furniture or dark? Or a mix?

- Textured walls or smooth? Painted wood trim or natural wood?

- Draperies at the window or nothing at all? Open, with lots of natural light, or a darker, cozier feel?

- A casual arrangement or a little more formal?

All of these details are clues and insights into your personal style, and to what you truly love. Once you start looking at your images through this "designer's lens," you'll discover that some images no longer mean as much to you, and you might want to replace some of them. Open up your folder of saved images and see if something else jumps out at you again. At any point, feel free to collect more images. You'll also notice that some photos already on the board are ones you love more and more deeply.

It is common to not want to change your board, because you put so much work into it. If you feel this way, take a photo along the way or at good stopping points, and print it out for yourself. Write the date on it and save these printouts in your extras folder. This way, you'll have each board recorded to help yourself feel better about changing it around. Your Vision Board is a tool and a process, not finished artwork.

This first board is still meant to be your "outrageous dream board," so don't worry about the cost of anything yet, even if your images are from the most expensive catalogs. Observe and take it all in. Start writing down any reccurring themes you see.

After you've observed your Vision Board for all the subtle details and have taken note of them, literally writing them down or typing them into an iPad or computer, then you will apply the ideas to your *now* home, room by room. I discuss individual rooms later in this book, where we will get into the nitty gritty function and magic behind putting together each room, but hopefully now you can see that you're starting to figure out your personal style.

The next step is to create mini Room Vision Boards for each of your rooms, which you'll be doing in each individual room section. There is power in doing this, as it is where each of your rooms really takes shape.

Action Item

ROOM VISION BOARDS

Your Room Vision Board for each room can be on a large piece of paper, or if you have the space, a poster board. Take a photo of your specific room as it is now, and pin it at the top of the board.

This step is the one that has helped me the most. When I can actually see my now room, I can automatically disregard the images that might have looked good in a magazine but have no business being in my room.

As you did for your overall Dream Home Vision Board, collect images you love for a living room, or for a bedroom, whatever the room is you happen to be working on at the moment. If there are specific pieces in your home that you already own and love, take separate photos of those, cut them out, and place them on your board. You can, and should, reuse some of the same images that are on your Dream Home Vision Board, but copy them so you have these images in both places. These images might take on a different meaning for you on your Room Vision Boards.

INSIDER'S TIP: I like to draw from my Dream Home Vision Board first, as I already know I love the items pictured there. At this point I'm still not concerned with cost, as I know I can get almost any look I like at a price point that works for me. Similar to finding an outfit in a magazine, there's always a way to shop that look for less.

When moving beyond your Dream Home Vision Board to gather additional images, include those that evoke positive feelings around how you want to use that specific room or space, the emotions and experiences you want to have, as well as the look you love.

- What types of furniture inspire you?

- What wall colors jump out at you in a pleasing way?

- Notice if the furniture arms are rounded or squared.

- Is there pattern on the rugs, curtains, and upholstery, or are they solid colors?

Again, at this point do not think about budget. We're just setting the tone. I can help you shop on a budget, believe me; I spent years focused on that. I can also help you break your budget! But for now, don't put any restrictions on yourself. Anything is possible. Remember nothing but pure potential for your room at this point. Collect multiple images of the same item. For example, experiment by cutting out ten or so different beds. Once you put them on the board, near your actual room photo and with your existing furnishing or new pieces you've picked out, you'll automatically know whether it works for you. Love it or hate it? If you don't love it, file it in the "No" folder. It's okay to have a couple of "love it" photos up together for a while. It will eventually become pretty obvious which bed you prefer. It makes your shopping less of a challenge when you have a few options to look for.

When I have a few "love it" photos of the same item at one time, I eventually narrow them down. I'll gradually, or maybe suddenly, see something about one image that inspires me more than the others. Looking at the Vision Boards and images frequently helps clarify your decision, which will save you so much time and money in the future. You get to grow tired of something on paper before you've committed to the investment.

Keep looking for images of more furniture and accessories that fall in line with what you already established that you love from your Dream Home Vision Board. If you're still working on the Bedroom Vision Board, for example, what types of nightstand do you love? How do they look next to the bed? Nightstand lamps? Bedding? You'll see your room take shape in no time.

Once you identify the styles of furniture you love, the next step is to move the images around the board in a similar layout, as you would place them in your room. This will help you experience the flow of the room, which will become visible right there on your board. One thing you will not get at this point is scale, as your images will undoubtedly be a multitude of sizes, and disproportionate to each other, but that's okay. For now, understand the pieces as they would work side by side in the room, and how colors or shapes will "ribbon," or move their way around the room.

For example, using your Bedroom Vision Board, pin the nightstand photos on each side of the bed. Do you want matching nightstands? Print out the image twice. If you want a bench or sofa at the foot of your bed, pin a photo of the one you love right below the image of the bed. This will help you start to see the room come to life, and better visualize how the pieces you are considering will look when used together. It is sometimes instantly obvious what looks good together and what does not.

The next step is to layer in plants, accessories, and anything else your eye is drawn to. Even add draperies or window blinds if the room calls for them. Try pinning an area rug under your bed. Do you like the contrast of texture and pattern? Pin up paint swatches for wall colors. Put everything you can think of inside this room on your board.

This is how you start to use the Vision Boards for your *now* home, how you want it to be. At this point you haven't spent any money, so try not to get anxious; we are simply creating the look and style. We're still going to set a budget, and a step-by-step plan based on your personal priorities. We're also going to learn how to repurpose and shop on the cheap, as well as learn where to splurge and where to cut corners.

Action Item

OBSERVE YOUR DREAM HOME VISION BOARD FOR RECURRING THEMES

Look at your Dream Home Vision Board at least daily but as often you like. Begin to write down on a piece of paper (or perhaps you've started a Dream Home Journal) any recurring design themes you notice. Include, if you can, the following:

- What colors appear often?

- What patterns and shapes recur?

- Can you describe the overall style? Do your best (but you won't be graded).

- What interesting or surprising details (dramatic plants, area rugs, and so on) do you see?

- Is there a fun object you love but doesn't seem to fit in?

- Minimally accessorized or fully decorated?

- Open and free-flowing, or cozy?

- Social feeling or more private?

- What else can you think of?

- Don't worry about your individual room boards yet. Those will come in future chapters.

5

Collaboration *and* Compromise

Compromise is not about losing. It is about deciding that the other person has just as much right to be happy with the end result as you do.

Donna Martini

Y ou don't have to demo your relationships when you demo a wall! Bring up the topic of moving, remodeling, or redecorating to almost anyone you know, and they'll share a story of a disagreement or battle they had with someone they love. Often it's over something so silly they are now laughing about it, but in the heat of the moment, that disagreement was huge. When you live with someone, whether your spouse, child, friend, or roommate, you'll inevitably need to blend your tastes and desires. For the sake of this chapter, I'll refer to anyone that might be as your "partner."

I've spent the majority of the last seventeen years in people's homes, studying the way they live, in the depths of their most intimate spaces. One thing I've noticed for sure is that when you embark on home remodeling or a design project of any size—even a task as painless as selecting the color of bathroom towels—decision-making provokes all sorts of unexpected emotions and arguments.

Remodeling, decorating, and making home purchases are all about expectations, hopes and dreams, and improving your life—not just your house.

Remodeling, decorating, and making home purchases are all about expectations, hopes and dreams, and improving your life—not just your house. Not to mention that sometimes decisions will need to be made on the spot, right now, and can't be put off. Plus money is involved. The right conditions for an argument or two.

When emotions flare up, remember that this is a normal part of the process, one that typically passes quickly. Finding common ground with your partner on home decisions is not always a cakewalk. But it can be! In fact, it can be the birth of a wonderful, collaborative project that can bring you closer together. It can become a source of experience that allows your relationship to build and flourish (along with your home).

INSIDER'S TIP: One of the most significant insights I can give you is that when partners disagree about "the sofa" during a project, it's rarely about the sofa itself. It's about something else, something key to their relationship. Chances are you and your partner come from different backgrounds, and various aspects of home mean different things to each of you. Neither of you is wrong or right. Understanding that these differences exist, and accepting and respecting your partner's perspective and values will make it more likely that you'll come to a satisfying compromise.

I had a client who . . . grew up with slipcovers on his sofa. His family would never allow the sofa's upholstery to see the light of day for fear of an inevitable stain! His wife's family was completely the opposite. Their approach to the sofa was one of plopping down, kicking up their feet, and curling up with a blanket, and usually, a stinky dog. It wasn't until we identified these differences in the way they grew up in their homes, and realized what a sofa meant to each of them, that we could move beyond their sofa disagreement and find common ground. She wanted a sofa they could really use without concerns of keeping it "perfect," as this symbolized comfort to her. He felt sofas were more of a statement piece as his family entertained in a more formal manner. She felt he was being too rigid, and he felt she was being impractical in every selection she made and wasting their money. Both had strong feelings and valid opinions on how a sofa can be used in a home. Neither was right or wrong, just different. Together we came up with a middle ground. They now have a light colored sofa, upholstered in an outdoor fabric that can take a higher level of abuse and still look beautiful. They are both happy, and they use the sofa daily. And their living room looks amazing.

I've learned so much about home environments and how they affect relationships from my dear friend and collaborator, Dr. Greg Cason, a licensed psychologist. He specializes in this type of therapy, and has spent countless hours in people's homes studying their living habits. From a recent conversation, Dr. Cason said, "There is no more important place for relationships than the home. Please your own heart, and you will have a long life. Please your partner's heart, and you will have a happy life. Do both for maximum effect."[10]

CREATING A UNIFIED VISION

You can overcome disagreements about your home, even if your tastes vary greatly. Vision Boards are powerful tools for creating a unified vision you and your partner will love. Create one together. Start big! Together, gather your dream-home images first. It's fun to dream together about your home environment. You will undoubtedly find commonalities in some of your images. Keep these as the base for your *now* home. Then build on those images until you establish a look that you both enjoy.

If you have kids, get them involved too. Creating Vision Boards as a family is a fun conversation-based activity that brings everyone together. The kids light up when they get to participate. It gives them a sense of ownership and excitement to help create a home environment where the entire family will thrive. It's amazing what you'll discover about one another and what they value in a home, simply by building Vision Boards together.

After collaborating on your joint Vision Boards, make a Projects List (see chapter 7) and establish your budget together (see chapter 8) at the onset, prior to purchasing anything or making commitments to contractors. In doing so, you'll achieve compromise with each other much earlier and will reduce the emotional, stressful component.

Vision Boards are powerful tools for creating a unified vision you and your partner will love.

I had a client who . . . let their kids create a Vision Board for their own rooms. This process gave each child a sense of caring, pride, and ownership of their rooms they had never expressed before. The parents even allowed their kids to choose the final paint color from a selection of three or four, and the kids picked their own storage bins for books and toys. The result was that the kids kept their rooms cleaner! Miraculously, the toys and books made it into the bins far more often. Even making their bed daily didn't seem to be so much of a chore as it had been in the past, since the kids now took pride in how their room looked.

COMPROMISE IS CRUCIAL

When you're remodeling or decorating with someone else, just because your partner's tastes and opinions differ from your own does not mean he or she is wrong—or right. This is where respect comes in: communication, listening, and compromise will set the stage for your survival and success. As Dr. Cason says,

> "Compromise doesn't mean giving up what you want. It means taking into account what the other person wants, then finding the place where the two sides meet. If you get stuck, remember there is nothing that will affect the happiness of your home more than the relationship you have

with your partner. Your partner's happiness will be the best design decision you have ever made."[11]

So when disagreements come up and emotions are triggered, go back to the Vision Boards you created together. Look at them and remind each other of what's truly important—your relationship, and working together to create a dream home you both love! Focusing on the bigger picture of what you want to create together, rather then getting caught up in the details, will help, as will talking and listening to each other's viewpoints as you discover new ideas and solutions.

I had a client who . . . with her partner was at a stalemate as to how their home improvement funds would be used. She desperately wanted a new kitchen, and he wanted a den to kick back in at the end of the day and invite friends over for sporting events. They both had valid reasons behind their desires, and neither one was being frivolous. It was a big difference in opinion. What worked for them was waiting until tempers cooled off. They purposely tabled the conversation for the time being, and scheduled time on their calendar for a *meeting*. This lessened the emotions, and each partner came ready to listen. They had such a productive meeting together that they made it a weekly Sunday event. It was their safe time to discuss an otherwise hot topic. In the end, they were able to compromise on a phased-in approach for both the kitchen and the den.

I had clients who . . . gave each other veto power over one idea they each didn't like. Each partner only got one veto, so they had to choose it carefully. If they absolutely didn't agree on a selection or expenditure, they had the right to say no without additional conversation. It lightened the mood and encouraged humor along the way, as they would tease each other about the veto power they held. Another thing they tried with much success was alternating decisions. If one partner got to make one decision, the other got to make the next one. This ended up working really well for them. The key was in agreeing on this tactic before getting into the heat of the moment.

There are plenty of decisions to be made during a renovation or redesign. Even if you agree on most everything, the one thing you disagree on can cause a big argument if you let it. Keep things in perspective and try not take each other too seriously or take a disagreement personally. Know that everyone is naturally different and flare-ups are normal—sometimes leading to new and better solutions and ideas. Compromise, respect, and communication are key to achieving your dream home together!

INSIDER'S TIP: When you live in your home during a remodeling project, expect constant disruption. Workers are coming and going, and your home is messier than usual. For the duration, your house will be a construction site, not your home, and being in it can be seriously annoying. Frequently people put off their cleaning routine, thinking, *Why bother; things are bound get dirty again.* This is not the time to slow down on your cleaning or organizing. In fact, it is more important than ever! Keep your circumstances and your routine as close to normal as you can. And know when it's time to get a hotel for a night or two. This break from the chaos and mess can do wonders for your relationship.

Action Item

- Establish a common vision by creating a Vision Board together.

- Identify your Projects List and budget together *before* making any purchases.

- When disagreements flare up, communicate and listen to each other no matter how much you don't like your partner's idea at first.

- Compromise: work together to find common ground.

- Take a pause. Table the conversation if it gets heated, and schedule a time to discuss it as if it were a meeting.

- Remember, it's never really about the sofa!

Part III

Stepping-Stones

6

Clutter and Messes and Incompletes, *Oh My!*

The object of cleaning is not just to clean,
but to feel happiness living within that environment.

Marie Kondo

We all have them: clutter, messes, and incompletes. The drawer full of junk, or the closet we've needed to purge for forever! Or worse, paying for storage for things we haven't used in years. My dirty secret right now is my garage. It's driving me crazy every time I pull my car inside.

When we clean up our clutter, messes, and incompletes in our homes, it allows us to have space for the good. Good things and good energy.

These types of areas in our home and life evoke guilt and unrest, and are not conducive to that *love-coming-home* feeling. Yet we still let certain areas pile up. We keep things that no longer serve us, and put off needed home repairs for some other day. When we clean up our clutter, messes, and incompletes in our homes, it allows us to have space for the good. Good things and good energy. This is true not only in the home, but also in life in general. We all need space for the good! It calls for a conscious shift in behavior and a dedication to doing things a little differently throughout your daily routine.

Ridding your home of clutter, tackling unfinished projects and mental to-do lists are an essential part of the process of making your home environment one where you can thrive. It's a process of freeing yourself so you can live the best version of yourself. It also helps your house be its best self. What could be more motivating than that?

I had a client who . . . swears she got ahead at work once she cleaned up her home. When her home was clear of clutter, she felt less burdened and more able to focus on what she needed to do to further her career. She was even getting to work earlier because her morning routine was suddenly much quicker. She could find what she needed, right when she needed it. No more lost keys!

CLEANING UP AND CLEARING OUT

Cleaning up and clearing out takes zero skill—anyone can do it. And it feels so rewarding! I always breathe a little easier in my house as a result. In fact, every member of your family can pitch in, and the payback is immense. When you clean up and clear out, it brings about such a sense of fulfillment. I actually feel lighter with each cabinet or drawer I tackle. Maybe I got it from my mom piling up things to purge, or maybe my days of cleaning other people's homes with my sister. In any case, now it's in my blood.

Whatever the cause, I know I can't get enough of it. My husband sees me moving things around in the house and putting things in the giveaway pile, and then he looks at our dogs, and says, "That's just mom relaxing." These days I find decluttering more than relaxing, it's exhilarating. Crazy? Not really!

Here are a few of my favorite ways to minimize clutter in my home:

PUT IT BACK WHERE IT BELONGS

As often as you can remember, take an item right back to its designated spot. You'll save time, and it feels good; you won't waste extra energy looking at it, procrastinating about putting it back, or taking time later to pick it back up *again* and move it. Have you ever noticed that movers, or delivery companies, always first ask you to show them an item's final spot before taking anything out of the truck? They spend less energy by moving something only once. It saves time and wear and tear on their bodies. That is, if they aren't delivering to *my* house, because I like to see an item in several different spots before I decide on its final positioning!

When you immediately put misplaced items where they should go, either to your giveaway pile or to where the items belong inside your house, you are giving yourself time for the things that really matter, the things that make you happy.

When you immediately put misplaced items where they should go, either to your giveaway pile or to where the items belong inside your house, you are giving yourself time for the things that really matter, the things that make you happy. It also relieves you of the feelings of guilt that arise every time you walk past something, thinking you really need to get around to moving it to the closet. This is such a simple shift in mind-set and habit. Try it for three days. See how many things you're tempted to leave on the counter or in a place other than where it should go. You will be amazed.

The thing that always amuses me is when I see dishes on the counter, let alone in the sink. Frequently the sink is used as a storage container. How much more work, really, is it to rinse and put the dish immediately into the dishwasher? It's so much quicker and less of a drag to tackle the dishes item by item, as opposed to mustering up the motivation to tackle an entire sink full of items.

I had a client who . . . challenged each person in her home to put their dishes into the dishwasher immediately. It took a few days to get everyone used to the new routine, but once it took hold she's never looked back. She now has a few extra found minutes for herself.

Have you ever mindlessly dropped something at the foot of a closest door? Try taking the few extra steps it takes to put it where it's intended. You'll love the feeling of being done! The same goes for taking something out to the car. I used to pile things by the garage door, and also on the kitchen counter. Not anymore. I take the split second to open the garage door, then my car door, and then it's done. Just like that. No more worrying that I might not remember to bring something to my office or to a friend I'm seeing. It's guaranteed

to be there, because I put it in the car right when I think of it. It will also help you be on time, as you're not traipsing back and forth through the house three times to get the things you forgot. I've been there and done that too many times to admit!

When you're done with it, or it doesn't bring a smile to your face, just be done, and let it go.

KNOWING WHEN IT'S TIME TO LET GO

Most everyone battles with the sudden reminder of how much they might have paid for something, or the thought that they might use it again. In reality, can you think of a single time that you really regret getting rid of that particular item (if you can even remember what it was)? Even artwork? I've been thinking long and hard on this topic and not a single thing comes to my mind. When you're done with it, or it doesn't bring a smile to your face, just be done, and let it go. You'll be surprised at how great and liberating it will feel.

It's interesting, but I must admit that in times of self-doubt or insecurity, I can be more prone to holding on to things that no longer serve any purpose. Pay attention to this pattern in your life. Watch your own patterns. Are you holding on to possessions in your home out of fear or insecurity? Or is it because you truly love them? Do they still serve a purpose? Do they make you happy?

I had a client who . . . was holding on to her great-grandmother's cherished piano. It had been in her family since the 1930s. The expense of moving it each time she relocated was exorbitant, and finding a place to live that could fit a baby grand piano made each move all the more challenging. She finally passed the piano along to her son. His family enjoyed it for several years, until they, too, had to move, and the whole cycle was about to start again. Finally, as a family, they decided it was time to allow the cherished possession to leave the family. Everyone felt a sense of relief, and this family heirloom is now being enjoyed by a family who needs it.

I can truly say that I've never seen a countertop **that was** enhanced by the pile of newspapers, books, or other **clutter** being stored on it.

OPENING UP YOUR SPACE FOR GOOD

I'll never forget the dust that would collect on people's piles of magazines and books when my sister and I would clean homes. We dusted these piles, over and over again. Every week! Nothing got read between those weeks that turned into months, yet we would redust the piles. And believe me there were piles! I always felt it was such a waste of my time. And a waste of space. I used to dread those piles week after week. Not to mention the guilt that must come from the person who lived in the home I was in, continually walking past those endless piles of unread papers. I can truly say that I've never seen a countertop that was enhanced by the pile of newspapers, books, or other clutter being stored on it.

Embrace the beauty of your home and honor it by not allowing items to pile up. If you don't read the paper that day, recycle it that night. Rarely will you would reach for it to read the next day, and if you truly missed out on some bit of news, you can for sure find it online. If you have a magazine and haven't read it within its published month, please recycle it! Have a "no more than one issue at a time" rule. At a minimum, tear out the articles that interest you and put them in a folder for future reading. Give the articles an expiration date, even if it is six months forward. Think about it. When you open up your refrigerator and see that your milk has expired (awhile ago, based on the sniff test you gave it), my guess is you toss it, with a little sense of embarrassment and gratitude that you found it before someone else did. Do the same for magazines, mail, and newspaper articles. Give them an expiration date. If you don't read them, toss them.

INSIDER'S TIP: Place a shredder and recycling bin as close as possible to the door where you bring in the mail, and sort it on the spot. You can open up bills, keep the necessary parts, and recycle the extraneous pages right away, to further reduce the amount of clutter.

One notable exception here is if you're saving magazines for your Vision Board. If so, also give those images an expiration date. If you haven't flipped through the magazine and cut out what inspires you for your board within a week, toss it! Flipping though a magazine for images takes three minutes, tops. If you're not already using your coffee-brewing time, or oatmeal-water-boiling time for some useful purpose, use those waiting moments for things like this.

Books also collect dust. However, books should be treated a bit differently. Collect only the ones you love and cherish. Have a designated space for them, one that you can dust regularly, as you would any collection. Treat them like the beautiful works of art they are. However, if they aren't precious enough to spend time dusting them, then that should be a sign to you, and the best solution is to give them away—donate them to your local public library or thrift store. Allow someone else the joy you had of reading them. And if you want to read them again, check them out of your library or purchase them in digital form. You'll have access to them forever, and you'll have more space in your home.

PRACTICE MINDFUL TIDYING UP

I've always cared about tidying up my home, but I would often tackle things
room by room or drawer by drawer. Marie Kondo has great advice in her book
The Life-Changing Magic of Tidying Up. She recommends tidying up by category. For example, if you have several makeup drawers, it makes no sense to
go drawer by drawer, as you might have the same item in duplicate in different
drawers and not even realize it.

Kondo suggests you clear out everything from every drawer that is in the
same category all at once, and only put back what you want and need right now.
Okay, maybe what you will truly need, guaranteed, in the next six months—up
to a year, maximum. Organize each category all at the same time. I've tried it
this way, instinctually, and I have to say Kondo is right. When I declutter and
tidy up by category it makes a big difference. I end up getting rid of much more
than when I go drawer by drawer.

A prime example: I had three catchall areas, junk drawers if you will, in
my kitchen for the longest time. A drawer by the sink, one in my breakfast
nook, and even a third one in my kitchen island. These areas used to be safe
zones for stashing junk. Junk that seems like we'd need it some day, but had
no specific place in our home. Note pads, pens, nails, scissors, old magazines,
folders, receipts, extra accessories. You name it, pretty much everything but the
kitchen sink was allowed in those areas. Those three drawers weighed on me.

Not the keep-me-awake-at-night type of weighing down, but it was always in my subconscious. I never felt fully organized or clean in my home. These three drawers were weighing me down with guilt.

Suddenly I could take it no more, so I cleared out all three areas at once. Dumped everything out on the floor. Organized everything by categories: paper, pens, scissors, nails, tape measure, extra keys, and so forth. I was shocked by how many notepads I had accumulated. To an onlooker it might look like I was afraid I might never have a piece of paper to write on, ever again! And then there were the pens. How many dried up, out-of-ink pens does one person need in their home? And my controller would freak out if she saw all those wads of receipts she didn't know she didn't have, sitting there in random drawers, waiting for me to bring them to our office.

Now I've cleared out the multiples of each item and pared down to only what my family will need within that year, as opposed to a lifetime. Maybe I've gained confidence that we'll have the ability to afford another pad of paper if we need it? Whatever it was that got me to get rid of the clutter in those three catchall areas, it feels great. We now have one area for each specific type of item and it feels so much better. No longer does my husband have to ask me where the scissors or tape measure might be. He can actually find them himself. We have our one drawer, and it has just the amount needed of each item. It feels so freeing. I can breathe better, just typing it!

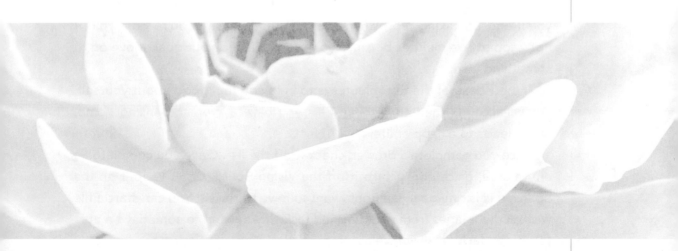

Action Item

When decluttering your own home, create a list of all the areas you want to tackle. Maybe *want* is too strong of a word. Pick the areas you know should be cleared out and organized. Write them down on a piece of paper. Better yet, on a Vision Board! Title the board, or your piece of paper: "Visions of my Organized Home." Add a room name or category to the board. And then under each room name or category, add a checklist of all the areas that need to be tackled.

Prioritize the areas. What matters most to you? What bugs you the most? Start there.

Then designate five minutes a day. Truly, five minutes. But do it daily, which I find more effective than picking one day a week, since you tend to dread that day, and it turns into such a big project. Plus, aren't habits, good ones or bad, created in eleven days or so? Try setting aside five minutes a day to start a good habit. You can even set a timer on your phone. It feels so fulfilling. The time flies by so quickly. I bet most days you'll end up taking more than five minutes because you're on a roll. If not, stop at five minutes because you accomplished your goal. Move on to something else.

The purpose of the five minutes is to help you feel good about yourself. You've accomplished something. Plus you have a more organized home, which leads to a happier life.

Once you complete a drawer, check it off the list. Once you complete an entire area, or category, take it off the Vision Board. Don't keep it on the board; this is one goal you don't want to have to revisit! You can start a file with all the images from your finished tasks if you want to someday be able to reflect back on all you've accomplished.

INSIDER'S TIP: When deciding what to keep or what to toss, keep only those things that make you smile. What does your gut tell you when you see it? If it's not delight, get rid of it. I promise you will be okay without it. When you pick it up and determine its use, do you think you will get joy out of using it? Don't overthink it. Pause and question occasionally. Are you being too easy on things, feeling too guilty for getting rid of something that could be useful at some unknown future time? I can sympathize with hanging on to your accessory collection, or whatever it might be that you've accumulated over the years. The guilt can translate to anything in your home that is still in good condition. For some reason, it is so hard to part with something that's still functional.

DECLUTTERING HOME ACCESSORIES

We won't even start into the whole clothes thing, but let's talk about your decorative accessories and objects. Accessories and art are tough ones and can oftentimes be kept way past their expiration date. When trying to determine what should stay and what should go in your own home, start by clearing a room of all the accessories. Better yet, clear every room of all accessory items at the same time. This is what designers do when redecorating a home for a client. It gives a fresh perspective to the space, and to each item.

Find a designated room, corner, or garage to gather up all the accessories in your home. As you remove each item, decide if you even like it. Does it make you happy? Does it bring a smile to your face? If not, don't even bother putting it in the gathered "keep" pile. Take it to your giveaway area. Be rid of it. However, if you still feel you kind of like it at this point, it's okay to move it into the gathering area.

Once you have all the shelves, tables, end tables, and counters free of accessories, walk into each room. Assess it with fresh eyes. Actually, "soft eyes," which you learned about in chapter 2. Do you even need accessories in this room? Having some empty space creates breathing room, a place for your eyes and mind to rest. Removing all the decorative objects from a room helps you really address each space, and each object, as if for the first time.

The reason I've had you gather up all your objects into one space instead of room by room is because I want you to look at each object with a fresh set of eyes and a open heart.

Ask yourself, *Would I purchase this item if I saw it in a store today?*

Even if you end up keeping all the objects, they don't need to go back to the exact room and spot in which they used to reside. Ask yourself, *Would I purchase this item if I saw it in a store today?* If not, take it to your giveaway pile. Secondly, is it looking worn or damaged, and too costly to repair (beyond something you can DIY)? Instead of allowing the tattered, unsightly object back in, take it to the giveaway pile.

Now that you have a pared down an assortment of objects, look at each item in the "keep" pile one more time. Actually pick up each item. You don't need to know exactly where each item will go yet. (You'll learn the art of accessorizing in later chapters.) Be sure each is a keeper. This is such a helpful, and effective way to separate the clutter from the treasures. You should now have a gathering of items you truly love. Big exhale. Doesn't that feel great?

HOW ABOUT THE INCOMPLETES?

We need to talk about what I refer to as "honey-dos" (even if you're the one doing them or are hiring out the work), because organizing incomplete tasks is itself a task. The leaky faucets, the unfinished baseboard, the broken screen door. Add these to your Organized Home Vision Board or your Projects List, which I'll go into in chapter 7. Keep the intention to fix these minor issues front and center on your goal list. Set a timeline for completing each to-do item. Better yet, schedule each one directly into your calendar. If, for example, you're not able to call a plumber to fix a leaky pipe right then and there, schedule a fifteen-minute time slot to make the call, and set a time frame for when you'd like the project to be complete. Doing so takes the task into action, putting you in the process of making it happen rather than letting it linger as a someday, guilt-producing, unfinished honey-do. This type of energy feels really good.

I had a client who . . . grew up with his father fixing anything that was broken in their home, so naturally my client wanted to handle all the light renovation projects himself as an adult with his own home. Unfortunately, he was starved for time as it was. Weeks turned into months, and the baseboards were still unfinished, not to mention several other things in need of repair. Even the dishwasher was tippy. Finally his partner could take it no more and hired a contractor to finish the baseboard. At first my client felt hurt, but later revealed how grateful he was that these tasks had been taken off his plate. His partner had removed a source of guilt that was eating at both of them.

You don't have to tackle repairs all at once, but do try to identify them in one sitting and then schedule the time you will dedicate to each task. Trust your common sense when it's telling you to call in an extra set of hands. Items left broken or leaking can be dangerous to your home and your health. They're not conducive to helping you love coming home.

ACTION CONQUERS FEAR!

Clearing out the clutter, paring down your accessories, tackling home repairs and cleaning to-dos—all of these tasks make space for the good. Many books have been written on accomplishing your goals and clearing your mind of mental clutter—the distractions that keep us from our higher purpose.

As *The Success Principles* author Jack Canfield notes, "Incomplete projects, unfinished business, and piles of cluttered messes can weigh you down and take away from the energy you have to move forward toward your goals. When you don't complete tasks, you can't be fully prepared to move in to the present, let alone your new future. . . . When your brain is keeping track of all the unfinished business you still have at hand, you simply can't be effective in embracing new tasks that are in line with your vision."[12]

We allow the clutter, the messes, and the unfinished projects to stand between us and true happiness. This causes unease, distress, and guilt, and can even harm our health. It's time to be rid of them once and for all. "Old incompletes can show up in your life in lots of different ways . . . like not having clarity, procrastination, emotional energy blocks, and even illness. Blocked energy is wasted, and a build up of that energy can really leave you stymied."[13]

Only you can make the decision to keep a tidy, organized home that contains only those objects you love.

Only you can make the decision to keep a tidy, organized home that contains only those objects you love. Getting rid of the clutter is relatively easy and the payoff is immense. Get each family member involved; they, too, deserve to feel that sense of satisfaction!

Instead of repeatedly saying, "I should do this" or "I should do that," take the first step of pinning incompletes on your Organized Home Vision Board. Once you do that you can say with confidence, "I am in the process of . . ." The action statement, "I am in the process of cleaning up the garage" feels so much better than "I should be cleaning up the garage" or "I need to overhaul the garage " or "That damn garage!" With this, you're taking charge of your life, your focus, and your home environment, where your best life starts. The sense of accomplishment you will feel by identifying these home projects, putting them on your calendar, and clearing out the clutter is incredible! Remember, the money you spent on a given item is gone. You won't get it back by clinging to the item itself. You will get more return on your investment by freeing yourself of the objects that steal your precious focus without bringing you joy.

- Using photos and notes, put all the messes, unfinished projects, and areas that need to be cleaned up onto your Organized Home Vision Board.

- Assign yourself five minutes a day toward addressing your incompletes.

- If it's a project that takes longer, schedule the time on your calendar, even if it's three months out.

- Whenever you are putting something away, or giving something away, try hard to move it only once.

- Rid yourself of the piles that catch dust.

- Have a one-day rule on newspapers, a one-month rule on magazines.

- Only keep books that are precious to you for whatever reason, including using them in your decorating.

- Remove all accessories from every single area in your home all at one time.

- Assess what makes you happy, what you love. If it doesn't make you smile, put it into a giveaway pile.

- Gather all the remaining accessories into one area in your home.

- Assess all the empty shelves and spaces to see if they really need anything at all.

- Look at your objects with fresh or soft eyes, and only invite them back into your rooms if you love them, and you know they are perfect for that specific space.

7

It's All in the Projects List

Success is the progressive realization of a worthy ideal.

Earl Nightingale

How are you doing with those incompletes and honey-dos? Are any of them feeling so big you don't know where to start? Accomplishing goals, tasks, and projects can seem insurmountable when all the details and decisions are swirling around in your head. Before you know it, "paralysis by analysis" sets in; you're overthinking everything and can't choose even one thing to do, large or small. It's a normal feeling everyone experiences at some point, but you can overcome it.

Before tackling any of your home projects, break them down into stepping-stones, mini-goals, or manageable pieces.

Before tackling any of your home projects, break them down into stepping-stones, mini-goals, or manageable pieces. This guards against the projects becoming overwhelming. Each project is actually a stepping-stone to your larger goal of creating your dream home, where you can be your best self.

You've already expanded your vision of your dream home through your Vision Boards. That essential first step drives your aesthetic and helps you identify the feelings you want to experience in your home. And now your Vision Boards will help form your overarching goals and projects. The next step is to get your projects and thoughts down on paper in the form of a Projects List.

TIMING THE CREATION OF YOUR PROJECTS LIST

You have already dreamed big—bigger than you ever imagined—and your Vision Boards are ready. You've set your long-range goals for your home. It's time to get into list-making mode.

By establishing a Projects List *after* your Vision Boards are complete, you'll know that the steps you devise will build nicely toward your end goal, piece by piece.

By establishing a Projects List *after* your Vision Boards are complete, you'll know that the steps you devise will build nicely toward your end goal, piece by piece. This keeps you focused in the face of emotional distractions, and saves you time and money. When you're out shopping with friends, for example, it can be hard to say no to shiny objects that might be beautiful in a store environment but have no business being invited into your home. Or worse yet, late-night internet shopping. It is so tempting to hit the buy button. Your Projects List and Vision Boards remind you that these sparkly distractions don't fit into long-range goals for your dream home.

You know it's *time* to start on your Projects List, but maybe you're not quite sure how to do so? Study your Vision Boards again, including the ones you made for cleaning and organizing. These are what your big-picture dreams look like. You've gotten your ideas out of your head and made them come alive through images on your Vision Boards, now you need to put them in writing.

At first, treat this step like a brain dump or a brainstorming session. Write down every task, project, and purchase you can think of in relation to your home. Don't worry about exactly how or in what order you'll tackle anything; you can prioritize it all later. For now, simply get everything you can think of down on paper (though that paper may be digital).

INSIDER'S TIP: Your Vision Boards will help keep your long-range vision intact. When you put all the pieces down in writing with this in mind, they will all fit into the entire puzzle nicely.

How often do you walk into a home that has a different theme or color scheme in every room? I can't tell you how frequently I see this. To me this screams of having no long-term vision, goal, or cohesive plan. It's a piecemeal approach taken throughout the house, item-by-item or project-by-project. By writing out your projects and tasks, and keeping your Vision Boards handy, you will avoid making this mistake.

INSIDER'S TIP: I prefer to keep track of my projects and tasks using presentation software, such as PowerPoint. With this method I can make as many edits as I want while I move through the design process, plus I can add pages and save multiple versions with ease. Programs like Word, Excel, Evernote, and Notes also work well.

The key is to use something other than your memory as an organizational tool. I use PowerPoint to track my personal life goals, so it's familiar to me. You can even use a regular spiral notebook. Chose a method that feels comfortable to you. One exception: try to avoid using sticky notes, as they are easily lost and can feel like clutter.

"Intention is the starting point of every dream. It is the creative power that fulfills all of our needs, whether for money, relationships, spiritual awakening, or love. Everything that happens in the universe begins with intention."

Deepak Chopra

CREATING YOUR PROJECTS LIST

A Projects List is another essential tool, one that is as important as your Vision Boards. Your Projects List will be the central document in which you establish priority rooms and categories, and then subsequent priorities for each room.

STEP 1

When I create my Projects List, I like to title it, and like a business plan, I add a mission statement to the front page—setting my intention for my home and how I want it to feel. It's easy to lose sight of your purpose and drift off in random directions, but your intention, or mission statement, keeps you focused and helps you stay on track.

Intentions are powerful ways of changing your life. Day-to-day, or even moment-to-moment, you set your intentions for how you want to feel, how you want to be, as opposed to going through your day or your life on autopilot. Intentions have a way of coming true if you take the time to set them—for a task, for your day, for your life, and for your home.

Intentions establish the "why" behind your goals. For example, your intention for your home might be to provide a truly welcoming and loving place for relaxing with your family and friends.

Action Item

SETTING YOUR HOME INTENTION

When you start your day with an intention, or any life ambition, for that matter, you bring meaning and power to everything you do. You take a step from mere thought toward something actionable. The same is true in your home. You can establish meaning, power, and direction by first setting your intention.

Think about how you want to *feel* in your home (and in each room). Who will live there, and what are their ages? (If you're single, and plan to be for a while, your intention for your home will be different than if you have four kids.) How do you want your family and guests to feel? Furthermore, how do you want your home to function? How do you want to use each room?

As designers, we call this step "programming." Good designers always approach a design project for a home by asking the family how they want to use the space, how they like to live. This is how we get to know the client and create a space that is uniquely suited to them. Overlooking this important step and charging right into the design process is like trying to execute a business idea without having a strategy. Or setting a life goal without knowing what you're working toward or why.

STEP 2

The next part of my Projects List is titled "Areas," which is essentially a table of contents, or, at a glance, all the areas in your home that you want to tackle. I even include the outdoor areas and the garage.

Allot dedicated space for each sub-area on your list. Set your intention for each area. Pulling from your earlier brain dump, list all the to-dos for that area, after which you can attempt to put them in order of priority. Later, when you set the budget and start to realize the investment needed behind each project or purchase, you might reorganize your priorities. Throughout the process, your Projects List keeps you focused and on track, making it less likely that you will forget about a specific step or element of a project.

As with any goal in life, if one of the stepping-stones is something you can finish without difficulty, and it's something you're looking forward to doing, it's okay to add it to the Projects List with no deadline. However, if it's going to be a challenging or not-so-fun part of your home project (for example, spot cleaning the sofa), give yourself a deadline and hold yourself accountable.

The initial listing process should take you thirty to forty-five minutes, tops. Please don't put it off because you feel it's daunting. Set a time limit so it won't take all day. It's actually quite fun, once you think about it as a wish list rather than a chore list of everything you'd like to have done in your house, whether you DIY it or hire it out. Remember, everything you write down can be erased or changed. And you can add tasks later if you forget them now. Just get as many of your thoughts and ideas written down as you can.

Celebrate your accomplishments as you check things off your Projects List. You've accomplished a mini-goal? Pop open a bottle of champagne, if you like! For additional motivation, it can be rewarding to look back at old Projects Lists and see how many things you've accomplished.

Here is a story of how one of my projects was not getting done, and how powerful and satisfying it was to finally get it underway:

It's embarrassing to say, but I once made a judgment call to paint all of our doors and trim white. We originally had a natural woodgrain finish, and I felt it was too dark. I had a variety of white colors tested out right on the wood itself. BIG mistake. After living with the various whites, we realized how much we loved the beauty of the wood and didn't want painted trim after all. Now it was going to be costly to fix—in terms of money, energy, and time.

Finally, I put it on my calendar—for a future date, three months away—but at least it was inked. It allowed me to exhale. Instead of feeling guilty and apologizing to everyone who witnessed the mismatched look of my doors, I said that I was in the process of having it fixed, which gave me great peace of mind.

So what went wrong with the trim project in the first place? Had I started with my Vision Boards and Projects List, I could have avoided this mistake all together, but I got overly confident and charged right into the project without doing my due diligence. Big lesson learned! The silver lining is that at least I tested out the white on only three doors before tackling the entire house.

Action Item

CREATING YOUR PROJECTS LIST

- Decide the format for your Projects List, and get started.

- Title your Projects List, and give your home a mission statement or intention.

- List the areas or rooms in your home that you want to work on. Give each area a page of its own. Title these pages, and add your intention for each.

- List everything you want to accomplish in each area.

- Once you have all of your thoughts written down, reorder the items based on your personal priorities. Remember, your Projects List is a living document that will continue to be altered and fine-tuned as you move forward through each step and phase. Nothing is set in stone!

8

The Beauty
of a Budget

Budgets are usually associated with anxiety and dread, not with fun or joy—or beauty, for that matter. But creating and working with a good budget that will help you attain your dream home is something to be excited about. Not something to be afraid of, or complicated. I'm going to show you that a home budget doesn't need to be frighteningly complicated; it can actually be quite basic.

Out of limited resources come some of the most creative and innovative ideas. Some of the best designs I've seen have been executed on extremely limited budgets. So don't worry if you think your budget is close to zero! That is a temporary situation; you won't always be faced with no budget. Many of the ideas we've already discussed in this book are low-cost or no-cost, and many more of those tips will be coming up in the next few chapters.

No matter its size, working with a budget helps you plan your priorities. It keeps your projects and purchases focused.

No matter its size, working with a budget guides you in planning your priorities. It keeps your projects and purchases focused. It also guards against getting halfway through a project only to realize you can't finish it, or that doing so would put you into debt. As with other aspects of your life and home, it's important to set an intention. What is your intention around how much money you want to spend?

Even if you have half a million dollars or more to spend, budgets are still important. The higher the budget, the more likely it is to become less vigilant about expense and thus burn through the allotted funds before the project is complete. I can tell you firsthand, as I've had a few clients who didn't want to have a budget. They wanted me to design and purchase based on what they liked. This approach, while fun for a while, eventually makes everyone's job harder and wastes time. These projects sometimes end up in disappointment.

For starters, without a budget, it's hard to narrow down where to shop and how to prioritize purchases. The client either experiences major sticker shock as project totals continue to grow, or they spend more than they should on emotional purchases and run out of money before completing the finishing touches that really pull it all together.

Budgets need not be lavish; I know for a fact that homes can be beautifully put together on the cheap. Setting the intention of exactly what you want to spend before tackling any project helps you achieve the result you want.

Budgets need not be spent all at once, either. It's fine to have a rollout plan— a specific amount you want to spend each month or each year. You've identified your dream-home aesthetic and environment through your Vision Boards, so you can be confident that you will stay on track to achieving your home goals, even if it doesn't happen all at once.

Comparing yourself to others is a slippery slope, and trust me, if you go down this path you will never, ever, *ever* achieve contentment or love coming home. There will always be someone else's home you think is better than yours.

WHAT IS YOUR BUDGET?

This is the most personal of all personal sections in this book. Your budget is exactly that—yours. Try not to compare yourself to anyone else who might appear to have more. This is easier said than done, I know. Remember, there will always be someone who has more. (Also, someone with less!) Comparing yourself to others is a slippery slope, and trust me, if you go down this path you will never, ever, *ever* achieve contentment or love coming home. There will always be someone else's home that you think is better than yours. There is always a more expensive neighborhood and a seemingly more beautiful home. But oftentimes, perception is not reality. I can't tell you how many times I've seen this with my clients. The most discreet ones are typically the wealthiest. The flashier individuals are often—but not always—in debt. I won't ever name names, but I've seen it all.

Near a place I once lived, a new home was being constructed high on a hillside. The owner kept acquiring all the surrounding lots he could, as he wanted to build the biggest home in the area—a quest to build a 100,000 square foot home. Imagine that! *100,000 square feet*!

For years we watched it being built. The first few years I watched with fascination. Then all of a sudden that hillside got quieter. Not much activity was happening. The construction came to a halt. The days of quiet turned into weeks, the weeks into months, the months into years, and finally it was sold for pennies on the dollar. They evidently ran out of money, or so I was told. They never even got to complete the home, let alone enjoy living in it. You've probably seen your own version of this along the way. Someone starting a building project they couldn't complete or buying a home so large they couldn't afford to furnish it. One's impression of another's financial situation might be completely inaccurate.

Based on what I've seen and experienced firsthand, the best advice I can give you from my heart is to accept where you are financially, and to be proud of where you are.

I've been in people's most intimate spaces for years. Being invited into someone's home as a designer, you see a lot. Sometimes we're there for several years. Based on what I've seen and experienced firsthand, the best advice I can give you from my heart is to accept where you are financially, and to be proud of where you are.

If you're not completely content with where you are financially, that's okay. It's temporary, life situations always change, and you will eventually have more. We're working with what *you* have now, not with what your neighbor or friend has. I've seen folks get into financial hardship chasing someone else's possessions or dreams. Please don't allow yourself to do this.

No matter where you are financially, whether your home is rented, owned, or shared, you deserve to have your dream home. A home environment that makes you smile. Let's make your *now* home your perfect environment, with whatever resources you happen to have available at the moment.

INSIDER'S TIP: If you own your home and plan to sell it in the near future, pick renovation projects that the next owner would find desirable. Try to keep things as neutral as possible.

ESTABLISHING YOUR BUDGET

You don't need to do it all at once. Please remember this! How much do you currently have to spend on your home environment? Write it down. This does not need to go up on a Vision Board for all to see. Do you have a lump sum saved up? Or a home equity line of credit? Or do you have a little extra you

can save from your paycheck each month? Or do you have a zero budget at the moment? Whatever it is, write it down. You can be resourceful with a big budget or no budget. This is the point in the book where you need to get real with yourself about what you can or cannot spend at the moment.

INSIDER'S TIP: If you're going to take out a loan to finance your home remodeling projects, financial advisor and author Suze Orman advises, "Tapping savings is safest. But if you need to take out a home equity line of credit (HELOC) or home equity loan (HEL), make sure you can handle the added debt. No upgrade is worth the risk of losing your home if you fall behind on payments. Interest rates on HELOCs fluctuate with the economy. This is a good option when rates are stable or failing and you expect to pay off the loan quickly. For projects you'll be paying off for years, a HEL can be better because the rate never changes."[14] She also recommends, "If using a HELOC, aim to have it paid back within three years."[15]

ORGANIZING YOUR BUDGET

Don't let this next word scare you: spreadsheet. Phew, I said it. For years I truly thought I didn't know how to read a spreadsheet. I've grown to have a great appreciation for spreadsheets, and now I actually look forward to reading them.

If you're tech savvy, there are all kinds of budgeting apps you can use. What's most important is to have a place to calculate the expenditures that go along with each priority room, project, and purchase. Excel can be used as a basic tool or an elaborate one. The type of spreadsheet I create for my home is quite basic, but it works. No matter which format you choose to use, here are a few tips to get your budget started:

- Keep all of your home expenditures on one list. (Don't rely on random piles of receipts!) Add your Projects List to the spreadsheet.

- Pre-shop before purchasing anything. Add the price of each item from your Projects List right onto your spreadsheet.

- If you have yet to find the exact item you love, add an estimated price range. For example, "one lounge chair $300 to $600." This will at least give you guardrails.

- Even if you love an item, walk away until you've assessed your entire budget. This cuts down the emotional purchases.

- Always get two or three estimates for a remodeling project, and add the quotes to the list. Keep in mind that the lowest bid isn't always the best option.

- Once you have all the quotes for each item on your spreadsheet, line them up in order of priority, taking into consideration what will give you the biggest bang for your buck.

- Once you have ordered your priorities, ask yourself: Do I have enough saved to accomplish all of them? If not, that's okay. Make a column with time frames that align with your budget for each item that costs money.

- Many projects won't require any money at all. Still, give each project a time frame in which you can realistically accomplish it.

- Emotion will at times take over, but try to stick with your plan and budget to the best of your ability.

INSIDER'S TIP: Budget 10 to 20 percent for overages. This isn't meant to scare you away from making your home an environment that is well suited for the way you want to live. It's to keep you from being caught off guard. From years spent on construction sites and observing clients' remodels, including my own, I've learned that it's best to plan for the unforeseen. Adding in 10 to 20 percent will help you weather any unexpected financial storms that might arise along the way.

DIY SAVINGS

At what point should you hire out? Obviously doing something on your own will save you money in the short term, but it might not bring about your desired outcome. Be realistic with what you can DIY and when you should hire help. And keep in mind the value of your time. Often, we think we can save money by doing something that ends up taking a great deal more time than we thought it would. Unless it's something you truly enjoy doing, adding in the value of your own time can render a project less expensive to hire out, not to mention the value of accountability and warranties. If something goes wrong and you DIY'd it, *you* get to pay for the repairs.

Assuming you aren't a contractor or skilled craftsman by trade, here is a partial list of what you might be able do on your own versus what you should steer clear of. If you have any doubt, hire it out!

IF YOU'RE AN AMATEUR DO-IT-YOURSELFER, YOU MIGHT BE ABLE TO:

- Establish your design plan through Vision Boards.

- Move furniture, except big things (pianos, pool tables, large appliances, and so on).

- Do light reupholstery work (dining chair, padded bench, and so on).

- Paint walls and ceilings.

- Hang artwork.

- Put up wallpaper.

- Add decorative items throughout your home.

- Replace doorknobs, cabinet hardware, and switchplates.

- Repair grout.

- Clean and organize.

- Make throw-pillow covers or drapery panels.

- Hang draperies.

IF YOU'RE A SOMEWHAT SKILLED DO-IT-YOURSELFER, YOU MIGHT BE ABLE TO:

- Paint or refinish cabinets, trim, and doors.

- Install tile flooring or backsplashes.

- Install engineered hardwood floors.

- Landscape (mowing lawns, weeding, and planting).

- Build a deck.

- Handle some demolition.

YOU SHOULD HIRE A PROFESSIONAL FOR:

- Upholstering an entire sofa (although my mom did it, so it's possible for a layperson).

- Electrical work (hardwiring light fixtures, adding outlets, and so on).

- Plumbing.

- Hard landscaping (building retaining walls and fireplaces, installing water features, or for anything that requires more than hand tools).

- Moving or changing walls, or making new openings for any reason.

- Replacing, changing, or building a roof (unless you're my dad).

- Installing or changing gutters—or even cleaning them, if a ladder is involved.

- Installing slab countertops.

- Resurfacing a pool.

WORKING WITH A LIMITED BUDGET

If you have a zero budget at the moment, that's okay. Believe me, I've been there. When we were growing, up my mom made almost everything that came into our home. My dad even figured out a new roof system that we could afford, and he installed it himself! Having limited resources makes you all the more inventive.

If you're in a situation with no money, and you wish you had some, that's normal too. Set a goal for yourself. What would you like to be able to spend on your home? Identify that amount and make it a goal. Set an intention for what you want to save. Then make a list of all the things you can do to save or earn that money. When you do this, it's amazing how you'll find money in places you never imagined. Be prepared to work hard, but also be prepared for money to show up when you most need it.

MONEY-SAVING TIPS

If you can't find items that fit your budget, then you know it's time to get resourceful. Here are some helpful tips:

- Almost every online and brick-and-mortar retailer that sells home décor items has an end-of-season sale. Spring and autumn are strong seasons for home products. If you wait for end-of-season closeouts, you can land great products, sometimes priced below the retailer's cost.

- Don't forget to shop yard sales, flea markets, outlets, consignments shops, craigslist, and eBay. These are great places to score unexpected finds.

- Can you repurpose an object into what you need? Will paint or new fabric transform an item into something you love? Oftentimes this is the case. If not, don't touch it! It's better to wait and not waste your money or time.

- What can you repurpose that's already existing in your home? Look at each item with a fresh set of eyes. Sometimes a new coat of paint can change an accent item that no longer matches your updated décor into a piece that suddenly works wonderfully. Try new hardware on a dresser. (It's amazing how this small change can help a child's dresser transition through their growing years, and beyond.)

- Most rooms in your home require fabric, and fabric costs can add up fast. Especially on windows. Many fabric stores have remnants from bolts that they offer at big discounts. The disadvantage with remnants is that you

might not be able to find that exact fabric again. Try to buy a few extra yards of it (or any other fabrics you need) to keep on hand in case you need to recover something due to a stain or other damage. And remember that there are also less expensive but still good quality synthetic versions of almost every type of high-end fabric. Do your homework. If you love a fabric but can't afford it, keep shopping. You will undoubtedly discover a lower-cost alternative that will look as good. Try not to get overly attached to any one fabric, as there are plenty to choose from. Fabric is one area where you can definitely shop a look you love for less.

- Say you are doing a light remodel and find a tile you love, but it's above your budget. Buy a few pieces and use them sparingly. You can mix it in with a lower-cost field tile to achieve a custom look.

- When shopping for area rugs, and you need a huge or unique size but your budget isn't big enough, visit a carpet store. Remnants from bolts of carpet can be cut and bound to the exact size you need. Typically the carpet store you visit can arrange this for you. Or try to find a machine-made area rug. The technology has come a long way, and this can save you a bunch of money!

- If you're looking for a new countertop and don't need to cover a large surface, most countertop installers keep remnant slabs from project overruns. I've asked about remnants many times and have gotten great slabs for bathrooms and laundry rooms at a fraction of their regular cost.

I had a client who . . . swapped home goods with a neighbor. Each had unwanted items that the other person had a need for, so they did an exchange. Resourceful!

INSIDER'S TIP: If an offer seems too good to be true, it might be. Try to avoid buying furniture at stores that offer you zero percent financing. They build the cost of the financing into the price, and you end up overpaying for your furniture. Not a good deal! If you really do need to finance your purchase, look for transparent financing deals so you at least know what you're getting yourself into.

INSIDER'S TIP: I talked about giveaway piles in chapter 6. But you don't actually have to give away items you no longer need. You can turn those items into cash that you can put toward your home projects and purchases. As with resourceful shopping, turn to eBay, craigslist, consignment shops, flea markets, and yard sales. I've sold furniture, artwork, and accessories this way, for my clients and for myself.

Consumer Returns

Many stores, brick-and-mortar and online, offer unconditional returns. Please do not take advantage of this with your home furnishings, beyond what is reasonable. In retail, you see a higher amount of returns at the end of the month due to consumers being at the end of their pay period, and wanting to recoup cash they might have paid on items not deemed as necessities in their household. By establishing your budget, and sticking to it, you are being kind to the world and the economy. Try to apply a 48-hour rule for returns to ensure you get the unwanted purchase back to the store quickly and without signs of use.

It's rare that the retailer, whom you might assume has endless money or is too big to notice one return, sees the impact of this; most often it's the vendor, the actual person or company making the goods, that takes the hit. Most returned products have to be destroyed due to an abused return policy. This affects the manufacturer's bottom line, of course, and their ability to hire or give raises to employees. Establishing your budget and sticking with it through responsible purchase practices should make you feel good, if for no other reason that that you're doing your part for the financial well-being of many.

Identify your budget and be proud of where you are right now. Don't allow what you have or don't have to limit your creativity. You deserve to love coming home just as much as your neighbor does—or anyone else, for that matter. From limited resources come infinite possibilities.

Action Item

PUTTING TOGETHER YOUR BUDGET

- Set *your* budget.

- Use your Projects List to build a spreadsheet for all your projects, purchases, and expenditures. Keep all budget numbers and purchase amounts in one place.

- Pre-shop to establish the price of everything you want to do or bring into your home before you make any purchases or commitments.

- Sort your Projects List by priority.

- Create a timeline for when your budget will allow you to make each expenditure.

- Adjust your budget or make plans for additional savings, if necessary.

- It's okay to delay some purchases as needed, but identify them and plan them out. It will give you something to work toward.

PART IV

Your Personal Design Plan

9

Eleven Designer's Secrets to Transform Any Room

*Some people look for a beautiful place...
others make a place beautiful.*

Hazrat Inayat Khan

While your Vision Boards set the tone for the aesthetic as well as the experiences and the objects you want to have in your home, there are also key *functional* design elements that make up each room. The design principles remain the same room to room, though the applications may vary. It's not rocket science. With the tips you've already learned, armed with the functional tools I'm about to give you in this chapter, you can create rooms that suit your unique style—all on your own.

When you enter a room that just feels right, instantly inviting and comfortable, often it's because there's an underlying balance or rhythm to the way it's laid out.

When you enter a room that feels right, instantly inviting and comfortable, often it's because there's an underlying balance or rhythm to the way it's laid out. It might seem effortlessly put together, but someone carefully considered how to place each piece. Everywhere you look there's a place you want to relax. The colors are perfect, harmoniously ribboned around the room. There is a richness in texture, for contrast and beauty throughout. Everything is in proportion, scaled and balanced to fit the room, and it all works together. The light quality is wonderful—not too bright, not too dim. There is a formula for all this, but it's not a secret! You can pull off these basic design principles on your own. It isn't a magic touch gifted only to designers. It's a magic touch you can learn to develop all on your own.

This section introduces you to the basics of establishing the function and intention of every room in your home: color palette, space planning, repurposing, getting rid of or adding new items, ribboning color, and bringing balance and harmony to every space.

Personalize Your Room Functions and Intentions

Did you go out and buy a big dining table set since you have a dining room? Just because you have a specific room intended by tradition to be used in a certain way, doesn't mean you have to follow suit. Functionally, of course you need a comfortable and welcoming place to eat. But if you have a generous living or family room, why not have your dining table there and use the dining room for something else? Home office? Kids' playroom? Make the room more useful to you and your family. Other ideas include turning a garage or sunroom into a workout space, using a living room as your dining room if you like to throw large dinner parties, or a turning a bedroom into a wine cellar or hobby room.

ESTABLISHING FUNCTION AND INTENTION IN EVERY ROOM

What are important elements in your current life? What do you need in order to function well and feel the way you want to? Do you work from home? Cook frequently? Entertain? How many people will live with you? Any pets? Do you have special hobbies or other needs to consider, such as sports, collecting wine, or whatever? Also, think about your dream life. What is missing? Are there activities you want to do at home that you don't do currently?

Think about *all* the details. For example, do you like to watch TV? What is the best room for that: the family room, living room, or someplace else? Do you prefer to sit upright, lie down, or sit with your legs kicked up? Knowing the answers to such question will help identify the furniture pieces you need to not only function, but to thrive in each room. By understanding the function and intention of your TV space, you can make the best possible place for you, for that activity, as it will be exactly how you want to use your room. It will be set up for how you like to live. At this point you don't have to have any idea of how you will pull it off. Embrace it by identifying it; that is the first step.

Consider your entire day, starting when you wake up. Include a typical weekday, your weekend, the seasons, and, if you have kids, summer vacation. Think about the activities you do often, if not every day. What sports or hobbies do you enjoy? Do you play games? Relax, meditate, do yoga, or work out?

How many people will spend time in your home on a regular basis? Your immediate family? Or will you welcome guests frequently? If so, how many? This determines how many places you'll need for seating. Don't worry if you can't fit in enough chairs yet. There are many clever ways to fit more people in a room than what you might think.

Do you have kids or pets that use the furniture? This will determine the durability of the fabrics you select as well as the depth of the color tones. Seriously!

I had a client who . . . chose the color of her new carpet based on a clump of her cat's fur! Not that she never vacuumed, of course, but she wanted her house to look good if she missed a spot.

Action Item

SETTING INTENTIONS

- Think through your day and list all of your activities.

- For each room you're dealing with, what are the activities you want to do there, and how do you want to do them? For example, do you want to sit or lie down while you watch TV?

- Be specific.

- How do you want to feel in each room?

- How many people do you want to accommodate? How do you want them to feel?

- Is the room for adults only, or are kids and pets included?

SPACE PLANNING

Now that you know what you want to do in each room, laying out furniture is an important next step. In times past, drawing room layouts used to be more challenging, but now there are many helpful tools available. You can also download user-friendly space-planning apps from the internet. (Two that are getting great reviews: magicplan and Amikasa.)

I used the tried-and-true graph-paper method with my clients for years and still use it for myself today. You can buy quarter-inch graph paper at any office supply store, and you'll need a ruler, a pencil, and an eraser. Let's say your room is 12 by 14 feet; draw a box on your graph paper that is 12 squares by 14 squares. One square on your graph paper is one square foot.

If you want a larger space in which to draw, and you are careful with your math, figure out your room so that 6 inches equals one square on your graph paper. That would make your 12- by 14-foot room 24 squares by 28 squares. Make your furniture cutouts match this scale too.

The point of this space-planning project is to identify the furniture you need, regardless of what you already have or don't have, and what sizes will fit in your room.

Before getting too far with the furniture, identify a focal point in the room. This will help you orient all the furniture. A focal point can be a fireplace, a TV, a view out the window, or a piece of art that you love. This applies to every room, even outdoor spaces. Identifying the focal point centralizes your space-planning efforts and helps the pieces fall into place.

To take some of the guesswork out of furniture placement, I'll share my favorite furniture layouts as we get into chapters addressing specific rooms. You can use these ideas as a starting point, a springboard for adjusting layouts to uniquely fit your spaces and the way you want to use them.

To be certain the furniture layout you choose fits your space, start by measuring each wall in your room and then drawing them on the graph paper as straight lines. Imagine you are drawing a stick figure of a room; this is all it takes. If you have angled walls, do the best you can! No one else needs to see

your drawing. It's only for you to identify furniture sizes in order to avoid buying things that don't fit. This drawing step helps eliminate the guesswork and will save you time and energy, not to mention the expense of returns. We've all experienced that nagging feeling of seeing a piece you like but not being sure if it will work. Having a drawing of your floor plan as part of your shopping guide helps you be sure that whatever you buy will work, and then all you have to decide is whether you actually like the piece.

When creating your floor plan, clearly identify all the openings, particularly doors and windows. Measure the fireplace, columns, or any other fixed element in the room and draw them in on your sketch. Again, I use the word *draw* loosely; just identify where these elements are, and how much space they take up on your floor plan.

Once you have your room sketched out, the next step is adding the furniture and accent items. Most furniture comes in relatively standard sizes, although you should never assume that; always measure items you intend to purchase for your home. For layout purposes, use typical furniture sizes and trace those onto the paper. What are these sizes, you ask? I have a downloadable furniture card created for you on my website, JenniferAdams.com, that you can print. Cut out and position each desired piece of furniture on your floor plan, kind of like placing puzzle pieces on a board.

If you prefer, you can also make your own templates by drawing out boxy shapes to represent furniture and area rugs, then cut them out and place them on your graph paper. Remember to measure any furniture pieces or area rugs you are keeping for now. It's much less work to shift paper cutouts around on your drawing than to move real furniture! Once you have your furniture placement to your liking on your drawing, solidify the layout by tracing over the pieces of paper you've cut out, or by taking a picture with your phone. This is a great way to keep track of your ideas if you can't decide between two or three layouts.

When creating your layouts, think about traffic flow. How will you enter your room and navigate each grouping of furniture? Will you have to walk all the way around the bed to get to the bathroom, or cross in front of the TV to sit on the sofa? Are the pieces spread so far apart that you can't have a conversation? Especially if you have a busy family, such concerns can be annoying and cut down on the feeling of flow in the room.

Experiment with your layout. Bring your seating close together for greater intimacy. Try not to shove all the furniture pieces up against the wall; floating items tend to look more interesting. Often, especially in smaller rooms, you have no choice but to place the sofa along the wall. When this is the case, allow about two or three inches of breathing room, as opposed to placing the sofa tightly against the wall, and be sure to have other floating pieces of furniture in the room. It may seem like that little bit of space shouldn't matter, but it does look much better.

Create your floor plan as if you owned nothing and your room is empty. You'll probably come up with a few different ways you can lay out each room. At that point, it's personal preference, and the best option is based on whatever balance and flow most appeals to you.

Once you have a layout you like, identify what items you need to pull it off. Does it require a sofa, two chairs, a coffee table, four end tables, two ottomans, and a rug? This becomes your shopping list. It's not often realistic to purchase every item you need on day one, so start by looking at your existing items. Which pieces will fit? Can they be reupholstered or refinished? Do you like them? If you don't like them but can't afford to replace them right now, identify them as temporary.

A replacement piece will go into your step-by-step buying plan that is driven by the budget you've created. If it's a sofa, for example, don't try to force new purchases to match this existing piece if it's temporary. Identify the sofa you love and build your room around that ideal future purchase. When the time comes, you will be all set.

Keeping your furniture layout at your fingertips helps with spontaneous finds, whether you're at a yard sale, a vintage shop, a traditional furniture store, or online. Keep a photo of your layout in your phone. Also, in the notes section of your phone, identify each piece you need and its size. This gives you a shopping cheat sheet. For example, you might write, one sofa: 82L x 40D for a sofa 82 inches long by 40 inches deep. When you start with typical furniture sizes and have your notes handy, it's less complicated to figure out if a piece that's a few inches larger or smaller will work without having to redo your entire floor plan.

At this point in the planning, you're not ready to start making purchases yet, so hold your horses!

Action Item

YOUR FURNITURE PLAN

- Measure the length of the walls in your room.

- Measure the openings and any fixed elements (fireplaces, built-in shelves, and so forth).

- Draw all of these on graph paper or into a digital layout app.

- Draw in the furniture you need using common sizes for each piece or the actual size if you're keeping something you already own.

- Once you decide on a layout and have identified those pieces you already own, make a list of the items you need including their specific sizes.

ESTABLISHING YOUR
COLOR PALETTE

Are there colors you have always thought of as your favorites? What ends up being right for your home might surprise you. This happens frequently when creating Vision Boards for my clients. I remember one client saying that she loved reds and golds, but when I put them on a board and showed them to her in a home environment, she felt they were too harsh and immediately knew she couldn't live with them. When I showed her a Vision Board that was predominantly soft sages, pale ivories, and grays she fell in love with it, and that became the basis of our color palette throughout her entire home. In the end, she had a soothing, tranquil environment that she felt comfortable in. She realized that the red tones she loved to wear weren't quite as appealing to her and her family in a living environment.

I've also found the opposite to be true. One of my clients said he wanted a calming, tranquil environment where he could come home each day and decompress from his hectic workday. When he saw a natural-toned Vision Board, he quickly realized that he wanted a fun, vibrant color palette: his personal version of calming.

Look to your Vision Boards to establish your color palette. What recurring colors do you see? Are they dark or light? What colors are absent? This will help narrow your color focus. No matter what color you think you gravitate toward, before you buy anything and try to live with it, make it visual and explore it on your Vision Boards.

As an extension of your Vision Boards, start collecting paint swatches, bits of fabric, leather, wood objects, whatever little treasures you find, in colors you like. It might be something you already own; take a picture of it if it's big. And keep these swatches and photos handy for when you're ready to start buying furniture, area rugs, and accessories.

If you find yourself gravitating toward a soft, neutral environment, are those soft neutrals cool or warm tones? Meaning, is it more gray or beige overall? Even if you are attracted to white, each room, and each white, has its own specific undertones. Are the colors on your Vision Boards mostly cool blues, greens, and grays? Will you be incorporating silvery metal accents or images of water, sky, or snow? Or will you have accents made of rock or stone, with warmer tones of tans, yellows, or reds and images of sandy beaches, deserts, and fireplaces?

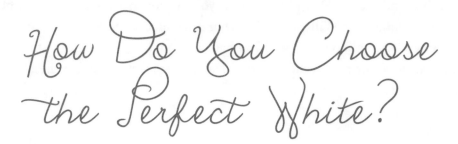

How Do You Choose the Perfect White?

If you've been to a paint store, you've seen hundreds of swatches. **There are so many whites it can be overwhelming! So how do you choose your perfect white?**

- Grab some of the white swatches from the paint store. Sometimes they have a brochure with a selection of their whites. Grab that, too.

- Then look to your Vision Boards. Are most of your colors cool or warm?

- Find a piece of printer paper and lay out your swatches on it.

- Can you see how some of the whites look cooler or warmer? Can you detect cool-color undertones—think blue, green, or gray—or warm-color undertones—maybe brown, pink, or yellow?

- It's okay if you can't see these color shifts; not everyone can. Pick the lightest on the swatch card of whites you do like, and test those in your room to see how they look to you and how they make you feel.

- For a calming feeling, choose a white with undertones similar to your favorite colors. For example, if you like warm brown wood and leather tones, choose a white with soft tan undertones.

- For a more exciting, dramatic feeling, choose a white with contrasting undertones opposite of your favorite colors. So if you like navy blue, a warm white with soft yellow undertones or ivory will look fresh and exciting.

- Once you are used to seeing these undertones, look for them in other colors such as grays, browns, blues, greens, and even blacks!

Once you have your neutrals, look closer at your images for secondary colors. There will usually be at least one or two recurring accent tones that you might not have noticed at first. If a number of the rooms on your Vision Boards are predominantly ivory, you might notice a navy accent that excites the soft ivories, or an amber tone in a leather, wood, or basket accent that gives an otherwise all-white room warmth. You might also notice other recurring colors in the artwork or accessories.

A good rule of thumb when distributing color is to keep the largest elements more neutral. Except for your walls, large elements such as the sofa, chairs, and major wood pieces are typically the most expensive and challenging to change, should you get tired of the color. Bold colors are best used in accents such as pillows, area rugs, throw blankets, accessories, or affordable art.

What color are the sofas on your Vision Board? You can certainly go bold and add a dominant burst of color to your sofa fabric if you like, but keep in mind that the bold color choice might be the result of a phase or trend, and something you will want to cover sooner rather than later. If you really want to go bold, consider making this strong statement with paint on your walls, because repainting is less demanding and less costly than recovering or replacing a sofa. You can also bring more of that bold color into smaller, easy-to-change elements in your room, such as pillows, throw blankets, and art.

Once you know your favorite color for your room, selecting secondary tones can be fairly straightforward. It can be helpful to look at a color wheel. (Search for one on Google Images.) If you want tranquility and calmness in your room, look to the colors directly on each side of your favorite color. These will pair well with your favorite color and will add a subtle, more textural interest to your room. Vary the lightness and darkness, too, for more interest. For example if you like olive green, and want to add interest, but not an entirely new color, choose a second green that is a little lighter or darker.

If you really want a pop to your color scheme, choose an accent color directly opposite your favorite color on the wheel. These opposing colors will add immediate and obvious contrast to the room. If you like navy blue, for example, look for orange or yellow to contrast.

Also, consider varying the hue—how bright a color is with how muted a color is. So if you want to contrast your navy blue, but pure orange or sunny yellow is a bit much, look for earthier or filtered tones such as paprika or curry orange and sandy-yellow tans, or natural jute or straw. The more pure a hue is, the simpler it is to describe, the fewer words you need. Purple is purple: grape jelly purple; what a four-year-old kid thinks of as purple. But you could have a purplish-brownish taupe or grayish lavender if you want a softer version of purple to contrast with your rich olive greens.

Think back on your intention for each room. If you want a calming, tranquil effect, you will be better off using colors that are side-by-side on the color wheel, without much contrast. If your intention for the room is one of excitement, fun, and lively activity, choose color combinations that offer higher contrast—colors that are on opposite sides of the color wheel.

Action Item

DESIGNER'S SECRET #3

Choosing Your Color Palette

- Choose colors that you notice recurring on your Vision Boards.

- Gather lots of paint swatches, bits of fabric, or treasures that have these colors.

- Review your intentions for the room, and choose colors that align with your wishes and make you happy.

- Colors are more soothing and tranquil when paired with similar colors positioned next to each other on the color wheel.

- Colors evoke a livelier feel when paired with a color opposite them on the color wheel.

- Contrast your favorite colors or neutrals with lighter and darker colors, either similar or contrasting colors.

DETERMINING YOUR FURNITURE STYLE

Choosing furniture is fun (especially for those of us who love to shop), and it puts you one step closer to your finished room. You did the math during the layout planning stage, so you know the dimensions of the furniture pieces you need. You've chosen your color palette. I've noticed, though, that many people still get stuck when trying to decide on a sofa. They think it will be the last sofa they will ever own! They might be so concerned about their ability to ever afford another sofa—generally a high-ticket item—that they take it way too seriously. But sofas wear out and lifestyles change. This purchase might be your dream sofa or it might be closer to your dream sofa. Hopefully, knowing this will smooth out your decision-making.

Let your Vision Boards help guide your furniture style choices. Trust in it. You've intuitively established a furniture style for yourself perhaps without even really realizing it, and it'll be a style you're pretty much guaranteed to love.

Start with the upholstered pieces, particularly the sofa. Among the items you gathered for your Vision Boards, what are the arm styles you notice? Do you see more pieces with straight, squared-off arms or rounded? Or possibly no arms at all? Write down the arm style you notice the most.

Now consider the overall body style. Do you have images of sofas with a single long bench cushion for the seat? Or possibly three individual seat cushions? What about the back cushions? Are there more sofas with one back cushion, or are the backs broken down into two or three cushions? Or lots of pillows instead of back cushions? Write down what you notice.

Now look a little lower, toward the base of each furniture image. Do you see pieces with exposed legs? Are these legs tall or short, metal or wood? Or, are there only small feet at the bottom of each piece? Are the legs covered up completely with fabric skirts that hang to the floor? Write down what you notice.

All of these recurring characteristics appearing on your Vision Boards help define your furniture style. Recognizing what you instinctually like helps focus your shopping process. For example, based on your Vision Boards and notes, you now know to look for a sofa with straight arms, small accent feet, a single solid seat cushion, and two split cushions on the back. Trust what you've chosen; trust your gut.

Next we'll take a look at the case goods on your Vision Boards.

What Are Case Goods?

Designers refer to case goods as furniture items that aren't completely covered in fabric: armoires, beds, nightstands, dining tables, wooden chairs, coffee tables, and end tables. Case goods are often made of wood and provide interior storage, like a wood box, or case. But not always.

Case goods nicely balance out the upholstered pieces in a room. On your Vision Boards, do you notice lots of ornately carved pieces? Or are most of the designs clean-lined and simple? Write this down.

What is your favorite wood tone? On your Vision Boards, are you seeing more pieces with a weathered gray, a dark espresso wood, or something else? Write down the predominant wood tone you see in your images. Also note if the wood finishes are distressed, possibly reclaimed and weathered by age. Or are they polished and more sleek in appearance? Write this down, too.

Now take a look at the accent pieces. These are the coffee tables and end tables—the smaller case goods. Notice the shapes. Are they square? Rectangular? Round? Or possibly natural one-off items such as tree stumps or petrified wood blocks? Write down any recurring patterns.

These characteristics will drive your case-goods shopping list. You can trust this list. You've subconsciously chosen the images on your boards for a reason: because you liked what you saw. You've established your personal style without even realizing it! And, you still haven't purchased anything. If, at this point, you're second-guessing what you see, your gut is telling you it's not quite what you love, and you still have plenty of time to change it. Vision Boards are a work in progress; they are meant to be changed over and over again. They are only finished once you feel they are just right.

DISCOVERING YOUR FURNITURE STYLE

- What are the arm styles?

- What are the leg styles?

- What are the seat cushion styles?

- What wood finishes do you see?

- What type and what color (or colors) is the upholstery?

BALANCING COLOR IN A ROOM

When the time comes for selecting accessories, consider color placement. Try to use a color at least three times, and in such a way that it leads your eye around the entire room. Designers call this ribboning. Let's say you like green and white. Maybe you chose white as your main color in your family room, and you want green in varied shades for your accessories. First, make sure that white shows up several times, perhaps in the fabric on your sofa and chairs.

Then, consider your secondary color, which is really where ribboning comes in. Clustering green accent pillows on one sofa but nowhere else in the room is not a balanced way to distribute color. Visualize all the people on one side of a boat, looking at a whale. To balance the color, have several green pillows in varied shades of green on the sofa and repeat that same color on the opposing chairs, in a throw blanket or in another pillow. You can also choose matching green accessories on the coffee table, and in artwork, on the opposite side of the room. One splash of color isn't enough.

Also, color includes the wood finish or material of your furniture. If you have distressed, gray-toned wood furniture, ribbon that gray tone throughout your room, too, in your pillows, accessories, artwork, and so forth.

INSIDER'S TIP: *Ribboning* is a design term describing the positioning of color through an entire room, leading your eye around in a circular motion. When you use a color at least three times, your room will look more balanced. This is particularly important with accessory colors. You can choose two or three accent colors, as long as they are all ribboned around the room.

Color also needs to move throughout the room at the floor level, mid level, and eye level as you are standing. Establish your floor-level color with an area rug, or large accessories on the floor. These could include baskets for a plant, tree, magazines, or even rolled up throw blankets. Floor pillows or a color band at the bottom section of drapery panels are more ideas. So is the wood tone of the feet on your furniture.

Mid level is that middle section of the room. It's not quite the floor, and it's not all the way up at your eye level. Bring color through the mid level with accent pillows, lampshades, and accessories on coffee tables, end tables, or sofa tables. If you have a bookcase, add your color there, too.

Eye level is exactly as it sounds, everything you see at your eye level and above. Artwork on the walls, tall trees, and your draperies are great places for eye-level color.

My favorite color is white. I ribbon that around my living room at all three levels. My draperies are white, as are my accent chairs by the fireplace, and the accent pillows on my sofa, which is across from the chairs. There is also a bit of white in my area rug.

My secondary color is charcoal. I ribbon that color in accent pillows on my sofa, the iron rod that holds up my draperies, the artwork above the fireplace, the iron legs on my coffee table, and in decorative pieces I have on my end tables. Charcoal is also the dominant color in my area rug.

My third color is a pale oyster tone. That shows up in the body color of my sofa, the bottom banding of my draperies, and on accent pillows on the chairs across from the sofa. I don't have this color specifically at eye level, but the stone on my fireplace has oyster tones so that balances the color out.

My living room is also open to my kitchen, so I ribbon that same color palette into the kitchen as well. If I chose a different color for the kitchen accents, the rooms could feel disconnected and subconsciously discordant. It wouldn't feel right. In the kitchen I brought in a large white clock with charcoal numbers as the accent. The iron pendants over my island match the iron in my living room. The kitchen counters have a subtle oyster tone to them, and the backsplash tile is predominantly white, with oyster accents.

You don't have to go to the extent of matching your living room color palette to your outdoor areas, which can completely stand on their own. However, if you do want a sense of seamless living, indoor to out, and your living room directly connects to the outside, extend the same color palette to the outdoor area using these color-use principles. Your outdoor furniture fabrics, finishes, and accents can all tie into your living room colors; an outdoor area rug can ground the space, and outdoor cushion fabrics can help ribbon color at the mid level.

Speaking of outdoor living, treat your outside areas as you do the inside areas. The same design principles apply when it comes to space planning: color placement, balance, scale, having a focus to orient conversation groupings—all of it. The only thing that changes are the fabrics and finishes, which have to be rated for outdoor use. You can use indoor items outside when you entertain, but remember to bring them back inside. It takes about one day for the sun to completely transform beautiful indoor fabric. I once used my indoor pillows as props for an outdoor TV segment and forgot to bring them in when we were finished. It took barely one day and my gray pillows quickly faded to not-so-nice off-shades of blue and pink! Always use outdoor-rated fabrics, rugs, and surfaces for items that stay outside and are exposed to the elements longer than a few hours.

Action Item

DESIGNER'S SECRET #5

RIBBON YOUR COLORS AROUND THE ROOM

- Use each color at least three times.
- Place each color in a way that it leads your eye in a circular pattern around the room.
- Remember the floor level, mid level, and eye level for color placement.

BALANCE AND SCALE IN A ROOM

Furniture, draperies, plants, and accent items all come in different sizes and shapes. So, confirming that it will get through the door, how do you choose which size will best suit your room?

Mixing up the sizes of items creates interest and helps you feel more comfortable in any room. Contrast your furniture heights. If you have a low sofa, try adding a chair or two that are taller. Or if you like to match your sofa and chair heights, add a tall bookcase, armoire, or large plants. Varied sizes and heights help your eye dance around the room.

If your ceilings are high, bring the room into a more human scale by adding a light fixture that drops from the ceiling, or by placing a tall tree in a corner or behind the furniture. In a tall bedroom, a canopy bed breaks up that cavernous area between the furniture and the ceiling, creating almost a roof over the bed, which makes the room feel more comfortable. Drapery panels hung lower than the ceiling help a room feel more proportionate, thus warmer by scaling down the high ceilings.

If you have low ceilings, hanging draperies right at the ceiling will give the illusion that the walls are taller, which can make the room feel larger.

If you have a large sofa, balance it with a large coffee table or ottoman. Or try a grouping of a few small coffee tables to create a larger unit. I found a distressed wood coffee table with iron legs that I loved. Everything about it was right, except for its size: a 34-inch square. I got two and put them side-by-side—the perfect size for our sofa—plus I think it makes the living room more interesting. The key is to find the right table that will balance your furniture.

Action Item

DESIGNER'S SECRET #6

BALANCE AND SCALE

- Vary the heights of your furniture.

- Choose tables that look right with your sofa and chairs.

- Add height with tall plants, lamps, and large accents, and hang draperies full height, ceiling to floor.

- Bring down a ceiling to a comfortable level with chandeliers, plants, and draperies hung lower on the wall.

YOUR BEST LIGHT

Lighting can change boring into extraordinary. It can also look chaotic if not done right. Your tips included here are meant to help you get the basic details of your lighting right. For major electrical wiring and overhead recessed-can placement, contact a professional electrician; these are *not* DIY projects. For more elaborate lighting plans, you can even consult a lighting designer who specializes in nothing but lighting.

For the basics, I will share a few go-to rules that really work, and a few things to avoid.

Several years ago General Electric gave me a basic lightbulb education so that I could be their on-air lighting expert for a series of commercials demonstrating how lighting could constitute a five-minute makeover to your home. This hardly makes me a lighting expert, but I would say I have better-than-average knowledge of how light quality affects your home.

The premise of the commercials was that the right lightbulbs could quickly revamp a room. At first, I was highly suspicious and thought it was a marketing gimmick. It turns out it wasn't!

Walk through your home. Take a notepad and count how many missing or burned-out bulbs you have. Then take another walk through with a fresh set of eyes. How many mismatched lightbulbs do you have? What does that mean? Start to pay attention to the color of the light coming from the overhead cans, lamps, and sconces. Do you see a rainbow of multiple colors coming out of your lamps and fixtures? White, off-white, yellow, and maybe even pink all in the same room? Do the same on the outside of your home. If you really want to have fun, drive through your neighborhood and notice the rainbow of "white" yard lights you notice.

When you go shopping for lightbulbs, there is such a sea of choices, even a whole aisle in some stores. Most people shop only by price and by a brand they recognize. What's more important is that you choose the same color consistently throughout each room and in each type of fixture, depending on the light you like. So, all your lamps in one room, if not your whole house, should have the same type of bulb; same with all the overhead lights, for example, or the lights in your bathrooms.

Are there one or two bulbs already in your house that you like? Jot down the brand, type, and wattage. Start there, and when you go shopping see if you can still get the same type of bulb. If that one isn't available, consider buying several new ones to test. Keep the packaging of your favorite so you know what to get next time. Get the right shape and size for your fixture, and if the bulbs are exposed, double-check that the shapes all match, too.

I had a client who . . . was stumped as to why the color tone of her living room didn't look good. When we looked up at the ceiling, we noticed there were four different types of lightbulbs in her recessed can fixtures. Once we corrected that by selecting the right bulbs, the whole space was beautifully lit.

INSIDER'S TIP: Recessed can light fixtures should always have triangular reflector bulbs that project light downward so it isn't wasted by shining up into the fixture itself.

If a lamp or chandelier has two or more bulbs and one burns out, replace it with a matching bulb or replace them all. There's no better way to kill the beauty of a chandelier than by mixing up the bulbs. Personally, I like a warm white bulb. Cool white can be harsh, and anything deeper gets too yellow. Different bulbs give off different colors. Mixing them up not only looks chaotic, it also changes the color of your paint, fabrics, and the overall environment.

There are also different lighting needs for different purposes throughout your home: overall illumination or ambient lighting, task lighting, and accent lighting. That sounds complicated, but it really isn't.

Ambient lighting usually comes from overhead, either from recessed lighting, chandeliers, or other ceiling-mounted fixtures. Ambient lighting also comes from your windows during the day. These sources provide general lighting. I especially like to have these types of lights on dimmers. A too-bright room flattens out the textures, creates harsh shadows, and washes out your colors. It can be jarring to the eyes and can even make you feel stressed or agitated.

Having the ability to control the light intensity with a dimmer switch helps you completely change how a room feels. Have you noticed how it's more comfortable, and that your food looks better within a soft warm glow at a restaurant, as opposed to the bright light of a cafeteria? A single overhead light in the middle of a ceiling can make a room feel dark, especially in kitchens, home offices, and other work areas. This is because no matter where you are in the room, and regardless of how bright the bulb is, you are always looking into your own shadow. Even doubling to two overhead fixtures helps a room feel brighter.

Try not to place overhead lighting directly above where someone would be likely to sit. Conversely, don't put a chair directly under a ceiling light; it casts harsh, unflattering shadows that don't do anyone any favors.

The same goes for where you do your makeup. Keep the light in front of you, not directly over your head. Lighted mirrors or sconces work well for this. If you need to light your counter, I prefer to use two sconces, one at each side of the sink, instead of one directly over the mirror which causes shadows on your face. Front light also helps for shaving. If you can't add sconces, sometimes dropping pendant lights from the ceiling works just as well. Using this type of lighting in the bathrooms made a big difference in the comfort and usability of homes I've designed.

I had a client who . . . wanted so badly to put a beautiful chandelier over her bathtub, which was located in a big bay window. I agreed that it would add drama to her large bathroom, but the electrician said no way. If it fell down into the water, somebody could be electrocuted! So, instead, we put her chandelier in the middle of the bathroom, over the floor. When she walked into the room, the chandelier looked fabulous—but without the danger.

Task lighting is designed to facilitate performing a specific task. This includes under-counter lighting in the kitchen or laundry room, table or floor lamps for reading, and desk lamps for working, writing, or hobbies.

Accent lighting sets a mood and tone. It also adds drama and layers to any room. Overhead lighting alone is boring, and harsh. Add lamps and watch the room dance! It's amazing how a lamp can fill in the mid level of a room and make it come to life. Sometimes accent lighting also works as task lighting, as can be the case with table or floor lamps.

Highlight special objects. Your art doesn't need to be expensive to warrant a major uplift with its own lighting. Look for single lights you can mount on the wall above the art and then plug into an outlet. The additional glow from these lights adds drama and dimension to your living space, especially at nighttime. Try hiding an uplight on the floor behind a potted palm to create atmospheric shadows through its fronds. You can also use accent lighting to creatively highlight specific accessories. I cut a hole in my entry table and put in a small LED light underneath a big piece of crystal. I love the sparkly glow.

Action Item

LIGHT UP YOUR LIFE

- Treat lighting intentionally, not as an afterthought.

- Be diligent about replacing burned-out bulbs.

- If it's a fixture with two or more bulbs, all bulbs should match!

- When shopping, test a few lightbulbs before stocking up.

- Verify that the light color output is the same for each type of lamp, fixture, and recessed can light in each room.

- For your overall illumination light source, install dimmers wherever you can.

MEASURE ONCE, TWICE, THREE TIMES

Before bringing anything to your home, even if it's given to you, carefully consider its size. How will you get it into your house? Think about its entire route through your house, not only through the front door, but also down the hall, up the stairs, and through the last doorway into the room. Measure the doorways, the hallways, stairwells, anything you might need to clear, especially the corners. One of my designers had a large corner desk that couldn't be disassembled. When she moved to her new house and found that it wouldn't fit around a corner in the hall, she donated it. Do you live in a building with an elevator? Measure that too! Elevator ceilings can sometimes be removed to accommodate tall pieces of furniture, but ask whether that is possible. Don't assume. This has helped me many times when designing for clients who live in condominiums or apartment buildings.

I had a client who . . . was not actually a client but the developer of a new townhouse complex with over fifty two-story units. The floor plans had a staircase that turned a 90-degree corner. The problem was the way the houses were designed (I had nothing to do with it!). King-sized mattress foundations couldn't navigate the stairs, even with the handrail removed. The developer had to purchase a new split foundation for every family who owned a king-sized bed!

Not thinking through every step of the delivery process, especially for large or valuable items, can be a costly mistake. You might lose not only the investment you've made in the purchase, but the time and expense it took to deliver the item to your home. So I'm going to be vulnerable here and share a mistake I made that was costly and embarrassing. Hopefully my painful experience will raise your awareness and keep you from going through it yourself.

My team and I designed a luxury condo in San Francisco. It was a corner unit with a stunning view, overlooking the ballpark and the bay. This client had a limitless budget, which is fun but doesn't allow much room for error because we could spend as much as we needed to meet the client's exact specifications.

My client wanted a casual vibe but with noteworthy pieces that really showed off his style. In fact, to share his vision, he had me fly to Las Vegas so I could tour nightclubs, of all places, to really grasp what he wanted for this bachelor pad. The final inspiration came from PURE at Caesars Palace. Although this nightclub has since closed, I'm sure this place was at the top of any designer's list of where they expect to get their inspiration. Ha ha! But it was a fun adventure. Definitely not a place I had ever planned to gain design insights, but it did give me great inspiration and clarity into my client's vision. He loved PURE's dark walls, white furniture, and abundant accent illumination—with a dash of the unexpected. Fortunately, no dancers involved! At least not while I was around.

My team and I touched every surface in his condo: kitchen, bathrooms, flooring, walls . . . you name it, we got to redo it. We even had the pleasure of designing custom cast-glass counters with lighting underneath. Every detail was spectacular. Then came the furniture, so we discussed how he planned to live in the home. It wasn't his first home, or probably even his second, so he really wanted this one to be fun—a place to hang out with his friends. He loved to entertain, and everyone seemed to love him. Frequently so many of his friends were over, weighing in on our design ideas, that I wasn't always sure whom to defer to.

The living room lent itself to a large, oversized sectional, in white of course, with the San Francisco view as the hero of the entire room. The sofa had to be deep for lounging and plush for comfort—but still modern—so we had it custom made to the exact specifications of the room.

We love doing big reveals for a client on move-in day. Music playing, candles lit, the lighting dialed in. Everything in its place. Then we turn over the keys. It's a magical moment . . . except for this time!

On the evening of move-in day, my client planned to bring friends up to enjoy his new pad. We had been working for days on the big reveal. Making the beds, folding the towels just right. Setting up every item in the kitchen. All of it. The final delivery was the sectional sofa. We already had the accent pillows, and could hardly wait to set them up as the finishing touch.

The delivery truck arrived. The sofa was still blanket-wrapped for protection, so we hadn't seen it yet. The elevator door opens, and the movers begin to put in the first half of the sectional. They put it in upright. It did not fit, but not to worry, as that happens sometimes. They repositioned. Still did not fit. Repositioned again and again and again. I was freaking out for real. In a few hours my client was arriving with his friends to enjoy the weekend. Not having a sofa was not an option.

The building manager saw my pain. He said, "You know, if you really need to get that sofa in, we could drop the elevator a floor below the entry floor and it can ride on top." Brilliant! Or so I thought. Then he proceeded to tell me that we needed a permit from the city and security present to do this. It would be a modest one-thousand-dollars! At that point, it felt like a bargain; the cost

didn't even phase me. As Jim Carrey says in *Dumb and Dumber*, "So you're telling me there's a chance. YEAH!"

A few hours passed and we arranged to have the elevator dropped and the sofa hoisted on top, and up it went. All the way to my client's floor. Another one hundred feet and we were good to go, with three hours to spare. Phew. The movers were dollying it down the long hallway to the corner unit. It fit through the doorway, and suddenly . . . it stopped. Stuck! It couldn't round the corner from the hallway into the condo. This was an absolute first for me. With all the furniture we had installed in homes, this had never happened. Ever. The guys tried and tried, and no matter what they did, the sofa would not go through the front door of the condo. And the way the unit was positioned, it wasn't possible to bring the sofa up along the outside of the building. Believe me, we considered every option.

To add insult to injury, I had to get another permit and pay another security guard—another thousand dollars to get that sofa hoisted back on top of the elevator and out of the building. Ultimately we had to have it cut in half, buy all new fabric, and have it rebuilt.

Needless to say, my client was not amused. No matter what he did to hide it, I saw the disappointment in his face and sensed the humiliation he felt in front of his friends. I knew they were all thinking, "Who did you hire, anyway?" At that point the music, the flowers, the candles, the beautiful finishes, the custom this and that—none of it mattered.

If that wasn't a learning lesson, I don't know what was. My immediate thought was to give up designing sofas, to flat-out quit and never do it again. Unfortunately for me, most clients won't hire a designer who draws the line at providing them with sofas. So I learned from that mistake and am now so much better for it. I have grown to love measuring sofas, so much so that I now have my own furniture line.

Let me tell you, that experience was beyond painful—not only to my pocketbook but to my ego. However, I recovered. And you will too, when you make mistakes. They will happen. Know to anticipate them . . . and measure! Measure again. And a third time! Measure every single thing you can.

MEASURE IT ALL

- Plan out the entire pathway from the store into your home before acquiring anything.

- Measure your new treasure three times before you bring it home.

- Are you having it delivered, or will you be picking it up yourself?

- Will it disassemble for moving?

- Measure:

  - Your front and back door.
  - The doorway into the room you are decorating.
  - Hallways.
  - Corners you need to clear.
  - Elevators.
  - Stairwells.

WHAT ABOUT YOUR WINDOWS?

I prefer a minimal approach to window treatments. It keeps things simple and saves time on cleaning. If I could, I would have all my windows and doors wide open, all the time, without any window coverings at all! I know that practice isn't for everyone, and I admit that more than once I've had to chase out birds that flew into my house. I do, however, like the look of beautiful drapery panels, which really bring the eye upward in a room. The key with your windows is to layer—and only as you need to.

Think about how much privacy and light control you might need. Besides their aesthetic value, or perhaps their insulation value from cold or heat, privacy and light control are the biggest reasons why someone would want to cover their windows at all. Are your neighbors close enough to sneak a peak at your dinner plate? Are there bright lights from your neighbors or from the street? Does somebody in your house work a graveyard shift and wish to prevent daylight from disrupting their sleep?

The best way to control lighting and privacy are slatted or louvered blinds. Plantation shutters, finished to match the window trim or in white, also work well. The bigger slats open wider for a nicer, clear view than the narrow slats of mini-blinds, but get what you can afford, and never leave dangling cords that could be a choking hazard for young children. Metal slats are better than lightweight plastic ones, which quickly start to sag. Vinyl can be less expensive than wood, and today's vinyl options look better than ever before.

If you have full-height windows, French doors, or sliding glass doors, vertical blinds offer the same light and privacy control as horizontal slatted blinds. Vertical blinds move out of the way, off to the side of your door so you can open it. Nicer quality vertical blinds have the bottom edges linked together, so they move around less if there is a breeze.

For a softer look, and if you need privacy during the daytime, go with a sheer white or off-white fabric. For sun control, roller shades with mesh fabric work well and give a home a clean, modern look. But just so you know, both sheer fabrics and mesh roller shades are worthless for nighttime privacy; when backlight by interior lighting, they are completely see-through.

While adding style and elegance, fabric drapery panels will provide greater privacy at night, especially when layered over a window sheer or roller shade. Draperies can be simple or extremely complicated, with lots of trim and details. You can make simple panels yourself or buy them in a wide variety of colors and fabrics. I prefer plain white or off-white, though sometimes I add a wide band of color across the bottom or the top of a panel as part of my effort to ribbon color around a room.

To make your window appear larger, extend your drapery rod high and wide enough so that the drapery panels can stack or hang on the wall above or outside of the window frame when opened. This also allows more natural light in and keeps your home looking tidier from the outside by obscuring a variety of colors and types of window treatments. The same goes for valances; to visually enlarge your windows, hang valances above the window, and only low enough to cover up a window line but not the glass itself.

If you need full light control, look for blackout roller shades. Some drapery panels come fully lined for this purpose, or you can have them made. Blackout window coverings are perfect for people who work graveyard shifts, travel regularly (and thus deal with jet lag), or live next to bright lights or a busy street.

CHOOSING WINDOW TREATMENTS

- Do you need window treatments at all?
    - What level of light control do you need?
    - How much privacy do you need?
    - Do you want a simple look or a more decorative one?
- Measure (and remeasure!) your windows before ordering blinds or draperies.
    - Inside or mounted shades and blinds:
        - For inside-mount, measure from the inside of the trim.
        - For outside-mount, measure to the outside of the trim.
        - For width, measure across the top, middle, and bottom.
        - For height, measure at the left side, center, and right side.
        - Remember, even a quarter inch matters!
    - For draperies and sheers, do you want them to extend from floor to ceiling?
        - Sheers should cover the window.
        - Drapery panels could be full width to completely cover the window or partial width for decorative purposes only.
    - Choose your hardware.
        - Scale hardware to your windows.
        - Match the hardware finish throughout your house.

ACCENTS ARE THE
FINISHING TOUCHES

Always save the accents (plants, artwork, area rugs, small end tables, decorative pillows, and the like), including your accessories (candles, vases, books, and all your various treasures) for last. It's so easy to fall in love with an object, purchase it, and store it on a shelf or in the closet, thinking that once you get the room pulled together it will be spectacular—only to discover that it then looks terrible out of the context of the store. And there you are having wasted money, especially if it is too late to return the item. Have you felt this pain?

That said, how you go about using a certain accent piece is one way you can break the rule of saving the accents for last. Occasionally, they can go first! If you have a treasure that you positively love, you can build the room around it. A great piece of art or an area rug are great inspirational pieces that can drive your entire room. On the other hand, decorative pillows rarely qualify as this type of inspiration.

Collectibles can sometimes be used as inspiration for a room. For a den, a media room, or another casual space, collection items can be grouped together to create a themed room.

I had a client who . . . was an avid Curious George collector. I'm still not sure why, but it was his thing, so his wife and I had to embrace it in their home. He doesn't balk at her handbag fetish, so she couldn't complain. And just as she kept her handbags contained to her closet, we kept his Curious George collection to his office. Gathered in one spot, it's a noteworthy point of conversation. If he had a Curious George doll in each room, the collection could seem strange and out of place, as opposed to treasured items that he had collected for years. Having the whole collection in one special place gave it significance, as opposed to one-offs scattered all over the house.

The point of accessory items—indeed, any item in your home—is to truly love each one. If you could take only one message from this chapter, I hope it's this: Keep only objects that you love, ones that bring a smile to your face.

When you are ready to decide placement of your accessories (adding new ones or rearranging), first remove every accessory already in the room. Everything! Even the items you are certain are keepers. You need to see the space free and unencumbered to truly imagine its potential.

Before moving any accessories back in, reconfirm that each item is something you truly love, something that makes you happy and will accent your home beautifully. If not, get rid of it. No matter what you paid for it or who gave it to you. Toss it, donate it, or give it away. Do anything besides putting it out just because you have it. I'd rather you sit with empty shelves as opposed to displaying dust catchers you don't care for, simply because you already own them. That's how clutter happens!

Add each accessory item one by one. Let them build on themselves. An object needn't stay in one place forever. I rearrange and question the placement of my accessories all the time. I have some objects I adore. When I think I've found the perfect resting place for one of my objects, a few months later I figure out a new way to embrace them. Sometimes I'll prop books under them, or add a clear acrylic stand to make them look even more important.

Books are great accessories and really help a room feel lived in, but only keep the books you love. Otherwise, books, too, can become clutter. If you're using books in décor, they don't necessarily need to be on topics you love to read about, but they should be appealing to look at.

I often use my books as color sources. My living room is white, charcoal, and oyster, and I generally keep the books in the same color scheme. Once, when I wanted to add a splash of color, I used hot pink books, a hot pink throw blanket, and pink agate coasters. That transformed my look in an instant and didn't cost a lot of money. Then, when I tired of hot pink, I didn't feel guilty about retiring that color and going back to a more neutral color tone in my accessories. When I want a splash of color again, I can quickly bring back the pink or move on to something else.

Books are the perfect way to add height to a short lamp or accent piece that needs a little more height. If you have the right size books but not the right color, try turning the jacket of the book inside out. Turning the jacket inside out instantly gives you a neutral, all-white look. This quick change can lend texture, dimension, height and a neutral tone without spending money on new books.

You can use books in almost every room of your home. I even place them under my most precious crystals. The books not only give height but the book covers' neutral, matte finish also contrasts with the sparkle of the crystals, or any other shiny accent item, for that matter. This contrast makes everything all the more beautiful.

Another casual, yet impactful way to accessorize your room is through the use of plants. They usually cost less than similarly sized accessories, and they provide focus, texture, and color. They bring oxygen to your home, and best of all: they're naturally lovely. The organic shapes balance straight lines and wood materials, and the various greens go well with all the modern neutrals. I can't get enough plants, particularly ones with large leaves, like the fiddle-leaf fig tree.

When you use plants as accessories, position them purposefully. Treat them exactly as you would any accessory, albeit choosing plants that will thrive in given light and temperature conditions. Try not to add a plant just for the sake of adding a plant. There are so many to choose from, and they're readily available, so only add ones that you love.

Some plants add drama—they look architectural, with interesting shapes and structure—while some are soft and tend to blend in. I put certain plants in specific places. One tree in a corner is not nearly as interesting as it can be if you layer and ribbon in at least two more green plants in the room. Repeat the plants as you would any other color. Try one on the coffee table and one on an end table. Another idea is to use several sizes of the same type of plant to create more impact. Think about a large "momma bear" tree or plant, and a smaller "baby" together in a corner or on the coffee table. Make smaller plants look taller by placing on a stack of books. Ribboning plants around the room brings that natural green color right out of nature and into your home. It makes your home feel alive and fresh.

There are a few rules of thumb to go by when placing and arranging accessories. Accessories look best when they're grouped in uneven numbers. Three objects, as opposed to four, or five instead of six. Vary the shape and the sizes for a staggered, more interesting effect, especially when they are a similar material or color. Grouping accessories closely together, in clusters, looks much better than when they are spread out too far from each other. And be picky. Fewer but larger accessories look better than lots of tiny objects.

If you have one single item and you want to give it more importance, try placing it on a thin clear acrylic stand. This automatically creates more drama for anything.

Dealing with Unruly Collections

One of my designers has a friend who loves hippopotamuses. Her friends gave her hippopotamus-themed coffee cups, towels, salt-and-pepper shakers, plates, calendars, books, you name it. No matter what, she truly enjoyed and displayed each treasure, but the collection was overwhelming her entire house. Here are some helpful tips to handle any unruly collection.

- Collect what you love! But display the entire collection in one area to give it importance.

- As with any accessory, group the items in odd numbers and vary the size.

- Display tiny items together in a clear bowl or vase, or on a glass plate.

Accessories also look better when placed on a contrasting surface. For example, a piece of driftwood on top of a wood table is lovely, but it becomes even more stunning when contrasted by a glass, stone, or metal surface. Or, for another example, a glass bowl or vase on top of a glass table loses its luster and disappears. Try putting a glass object on top of a wooden table, and watch it come to life.

When selecting accent pillows and throw blankets, the same principle of contrast applies. A leather pillow, on a leather sofa gets lost, and doesn't really add any interest. Instead, using a soft, nubby fabric, like a velvet or suede pillow contrasts the smooth leather sofa and is much more inviting. And bolder, fluffier textures make a linen sofa all the more appealing. If you have a plush chenille sofa, reduce the textures on your pillows. That's when you might opt for pillows made of leather or a smooth fabric, even a silk. Another nubby fabric on top of the plush fabric looks heavy.

I've said it before, only keep accessories that you love, that bring you happiness. You don't have to think too long and hard about this. In fact, it's best if you don't. It's an automatic feeling or knowing that you will have when you hold and gaze at the object. Love it or toss it. It's that simple. If you don't love something, no matter how expensive it was or if it was a gift, it's clutter.

Paying attention to this feeling is also helpful when you are shopping. Have you ever run across something that stops you in your tracks and you can't take your eyes off it? Or, if you don't buy something but continue to think about it often over the next two or three days, you had better go back and get it!

To accessorize my own home, I'm drawn toward elements from nature. I love crystals, minerals, rocks, plants, driftwood, and petrified wood. They give me energy in a way that I can't really explain; I just know it when I see and feel them. I also love books and unique objects that I've collected along the way.

What inspires you? Not what inspires your neighbor or what inspires me, what do you love? Those are the accessories to bring into your home. If dried or fresh flowers do it for you, then bring in more of those. Pictures of your kids, your travels, items that remind you of a happy moment, or a piece of art or a treasure you found on a trip. All of these are great additions that help make a house a home.

Accessories are the finishing touches that pull it all together and can really show off your personality. They don't have to be expensive items. What is most important is that they make you smile. If you love candles, by all means bring in lots of them. Accessories are treasures; they should be chosen carefully.

INSIDER'S TIP: Candles look best when grouped with like-colored candles. Mixing and matching the colors can make candles look more like clutter. As you would with any accessory, vary the height and the shape of the like-colored candles to pull off an intentional look.

Please only allow items into your home that will make your environment feel exactly how you want it to feel. It is your home, after all! It's the one

environment you get to control. I've learned the power that my environment plays in all aspects of my life, and I now choose joy over guilt! Once you try it, you will find it's an exhilarating feeling.

Action Item

DECIDING WHICH ACCESSORIES STAY

- Only keep accessories you love and that bring you joy. *What things inspire you?*

- Group accessories in uneven numbers.

- Choose items in varied heights, shapes, and sizes.

- Layer accessories by using books, plates, bowls, and so forth under other items.

- Contrast the finish of accessories that are next to or on top of one another.

EVERY ROOM NEEDS PAINT

One DIY activity that will make a big difference is to paint. Painting is the least complicated way to refresh a room, but because painted surfaces—your walls and ceiling—take up roughly 60 percent of your room, choose paint wisely. The best advice I can give you is to try to avoid being impulsive with paint. That's a tough one to follow, I know, as many painting projects are spontaneous. You have a free weekend, and a sudden burst of Pinterest-fueled inspiration leads you to stay up till midnight and get it done. I've been there! It's a great feeling. I admire and love that passion when I see it in others.

I've embarked on many weekend projects with this same fervor. I've also followed that weekend's passion painting project with another weekend spent painting over my last weekend's masterpiece gone wrong. Or I forget to take into account how much prep time I need and a weekend project turns into a three-week project. Even after all these years of selecting paint colors for clients, if I don't follow these next steps in my personal paint selection, I'm bound to make color mistakes in my home.

Avoid buying paint off a swatch you found at the paint store without first taking that swatch home. In fact, take several swatches home. Double check with your color palette from your Vision Boards. What might seem like a beautiful off-white or light blue in the store could be totally different when you get that swatch home! Observe the swatches in all types of light. Morning, afternoon, evening, late evening, and, if possible, during different weather conditions. Move the swatches around the room because rooms have shadows. One wall will take the paint color differently from another wall. The tint of your windows and your lightbulbs will affect the paint color, too.

Once you've narrowed it to your top two or three choices, buy small cans of each color. Use separate paint brushes or sponges for each color, unless (completely unlike me), you have the patience to wash and dry one brush between the application of each color. Using a brush with residue from another color will skew the new color, and you'll be in for a surprise when you go to paint the entire room. Go through the same exercise you went through with the swatches. Paint large areas in several parts of the room, maybe even a corner or next to some trim. See how the colors change in different lights. Choose your color wisely, but also go about it unapologetically. It's not hard to fix, should you make a choice that doesn't work for you.

Beyond the paint color, choosing the right paint finish for the surface matters too. Most manufacturers have four or five sheens including: flat, eggshell, satin, semigloss, and gloss. Here are some general guidelines:

- Ceilings: Choose flat because you don't have to clean ceilings often, and a flat finish doesn't reflect the light.

- Walls: Use eggshell for most living spaces because it is more durable than flat yet still has a soft finish. Satin is easier to wash and clean, and it works better for hardworking kitchens, bathrooms, and sometimes kids' rooms. However, if you have a room that gets plenty of sunlight, a shinier paint finish, like a satin, can turn into a mirror, as it is more reflective.

- Trim: Semigloss is good for trim, but I prefer gloss, which is the hardest, most durable paint finish. If you really want a strong finish, look for enamel paint. It's not as forgiving to apply, so you might need different brushes or paint thinner for cleanup.

Action Item

REFRESH WITH PAINT

- Test several color swatches in different light conditions in your home before buying paint.

- Invest in small cans of paint to test on the walls after identifying possible color choices from the swatches. View in various lights.

- Choose the right paint finish for each surface.

10

Gathering Spaces: From Your Living Room to Your Kitchen

This is the power of gathering: It inspires us—delightfully—to be more hopeful, more joyful, more thoughtful; in a word, more alive.

Alice Waters

Now is the time to actually design a room! So far in this book you've read about the basic elements of design and determined the style of your home through your Dream Home Vision Board. You've set your intentions for your entire home and have started your Projects List. You've learned about color, furniture, accessorizing, and all the pieces that go into your rooms. You've learned about the not-so-obvious elements that affect all of your senses, too, including your sixth sense, your intuition. All this will come in handy again and again as your Personal Design Plan for each room comes to life.

This chapter acts as your reference guide as you enter into each specific room of your home. We will focus on gathering rooms—living and family rooms—and feasting rooms—dining rooms and kitchens. You don't have to read each room section all at once. You can read each specific room as you are ready to tackle that particular space in your home.

INSIDER'S TIP: Are there activities that you want to do, but they aren't assigned a room yet? You might have activities such as eating that take place in several rooms. Read through the sections addressing those activities. For example, if you want to redo your family room to be meal-friendly, even if you want to have most of your meals at your kitchen table, get started by reading the sections on gathering rooms and where you feast.

GATHERING ROOMS:
INSIDE AND OUT

Gathering rooms can be traditional living rooms, family rooms, great rooms, dens, and even your outdoor seating areas, wherever you want to sit and read, talk or relax, socialize and entertain. It's probably where you spend most of your time at home, if you're not sleeping, cooking, or working.

The magic of a highly social gathering room is how everyone can find a comfortable place for whatever they want to do, and still be with the rest of the family, roommates, or friends even if they're not actively engaging each other. It's ideally a space that's casually inviting and effortless, with carefree, durable, stain-resistant fabrics, and versatile furniture that can be for lively or casual conversation, or even a kids' play area.

START BY SETTING YOUR INTENTION

Do you have one gathering room, or possibly two if you include your outdoor space? Start by setting your intention for how you want to use each space. It's okay if the intention behind each gathering area is identical, and it's also okay if your intention for how you use each gathering space is completely opposite. The most important thing is to think through exactly how you and your family like to live. And don't compromise when you set your intention. If all you have is pure potential in your gathering room, how do you want to use it? What mood do you want to create? This will shape all the decisions you make in relation to the room.

Get specific. How many people do you want in your gathering room at any one time? Don't limit yourself by how many seating spaces you've had in the past. There are creative ways to fit in additional seating that you might not have thought of yet.

If there's a TV in the room, do you like to watch it sitting upright or lying down? This will shape the style of furniture you choose. Who will be using your room? Only adults, or will it be a mix of kids and fur babies? This will shape your fabric decisions. And how do you want to feel in the room? Relaxed and calm, or upbeat and lively? All of this will help focus your color choices and accent items.

WHAT IS THE FOCUS?

Every successful room needs a focal point. The focal point might be the TV, a fireplace, or something else, like a beautiful view. Make certain you can see the primary focus as you enter the room. For outdoor spaces, maybe the focus is also a fire pit, pizza oven, water feature, beautiful tree, or swimming pool. Orient your furniture to take advantage of this focus, but not so much that it puts the back of all your furniture to the entry of this room. If you don't have an obvious focus, create one with a large piece of furniture such as an armoire or media shelves and your TV. This will organize your room and will help you place your furniture.

LAY OUT YOUR FURNITURE

First, lay out your furniture on graph paper, large items first. Anchor the room with the sofa, coffee table, and two or three larger chairs. Add some lightweight stools or a bench as seating that can be moved without difficulty. A sectional with no arms functions like a bench, and somebody can sit toward the main part of the sofa or outward, to talk with different groups. And, to create a welcoming feel, orient the furniture so you can walk right in and sit down. If you have young kids, lightweight, soft ottomans can be used as your coffee table, so you can move them to create a big open space in the center for play.

An ottoman or coffee table you can sit on is great for quick conversations, but nobody wants to be in the middle of the seating group for long. If you have kids, get a lightweight coffee table or one on wheels, so it can move out of the way for a play area. Or use three or four smaller tables, or stools, that go together to make a larger table.

ADD YOUR ACCENT FURNITURE

Your accent furniture bridges the gap between your major pieces and your accessories. Accents can be inexpensive and more colorful, if you like to change your look often, or they can match your sofa and chairs; it's up to you. Flexible seating options can be fun accents, especially when they are not hard to move around. Stools, benches, poufs, floor pillows, pull-up side chairs, garden stools, wood blocks, and so on are versatile and attractive. These also double as little side tables when you are entertaining, if they have a firm, flat surface that won't tip.

Provide a place to set a drink or a book, within reach of every seat. End tables are great for this, especially when the coffee table is a little too far from the chairs. The floor doesn't count as a place to put a drink! Neither does a soft ottoman or stool, unless there is a sturdy tray on top that won't tip. Depending on your sofa placement and the size of your room, a taller table, narrow cabinet, low bookcase, or a bench behind your sofa is a nice touch. Coffee tables should always be centered to the sofa, and within close reach—no more than eighteen inches away.

AREA RUGS

Even if you have carpet, area rugs are the best way to anchor any furniture grouping and, therefore, your entire room. But it's really common to choose a rug that's too small. Most rugs come in standard sizes, but, often, that has nothing to do with the sizes of rooms. The standard sizes for rugs are, in feet: nine by twelve, eight by ten, five by seven, four by six, three by four (or five), and two by three. Sometimes you'll find a size that is close to these. If you're looking for a special size that will really make your room perfect, you might be better off ordering a custom-made rug or spending the time shopping for something unique and handmade.

The only real rule for area rugs, especially if you have a wood or stone floor: Always have an even number of furniture feet on the rug. This means no feet, two feet, or all the feet. Most furniture pieces have four feet, so never have one or three on the rug, because then that chair or whatever will rock a little. Now that I've said the word *never*, I admit to putting a sticky felt pad under a single foot on a lounge chair, because that placement was a little unusual for the room this client had. The chair really needed to be at an angle to suit the room, and no matter how hard I tried, I could not get all four legs to fit on the rug.

LIGHTING

Beyond whatever lighting is built into your house, additional lighting will help you set the mood and make your room feel more intimate, relaxing, or festive. Boring overhead lights rarely create an inviting atmosphere. If your ceilings are high, attractive chandeliers are a better option, especially if they are controlled by a dimmer switch. Chandeliers bring the tall space down to a more comfortable human scale and add a decorative touch. Floor lamps and lamps on tables help make the space look finished.

For gathering rooms, try to have a lamp of some sort at both ends of your sofa, or between groupings of two chairs. The idea is that someone could have nice light for reading, wherever they are: a floor lamp on one end and a lamp on an end table at the other end, or a pair of lamps on end tables. Overall, use the same lightbulb in all of the lamps for a consistent light quality. And spotlight

big plants or artwork with lighting made for this. It will reinforce your focal feature any time of day, and add interest at nighttime.

WINDOW TREATMENTS

Do you really need window treatments? A gathering room is already a social space, so you might not need as much privacy as you would in a bedroom or bathroom. But you might need to control the sunlight to reduce glare on a TV or to shade the room from the heat of summer.

A minimal approach to window treatments in gathering rooms works well, unless you prefer a more formal look. Simple is more modern, and conversely, using lots of layers tends to give a room a more formal look. Neither is right or wrong; it all goes back to the intention you want to set for the room.

Plantation shutters or basic drapery panels work well in social areas of a house if you need something on the windows. Windows in these rooms are often quite large, and heavy fabrics in dark colors can feel overwhelming in the summer but cozy in winter.

ESTABLISHING YOUR PALETTE

Keep your home's overall color palette in mind (see chapter 9), but feel free to mix things up a little, room by room, as long as your entire home has a consistent feel to it. Keep the colors of your ceilings, trim, and flooring the same throughout, for the most part. This will give your home a tied-together appearance even if you opt to vary the color of the walls.

If you enjoy bright colors, gathering rooms, since they are social, active rooms, can use some of the brighter colors in your palette, especially as accents for a livelier effect. But, again, this goes back to your intention for the room. If your intention is to have a tranquil gathering room, you might want to opt for white or very light walls with extra texture for interest, as opposed to bright accent colors. Look again at your overall color palette and the Vision Board you created for this room. What do you see? On the walls, for example, do you notice bright colors, or more subdued? Use this as your cue for establishing your color palette. Stay within your comfort level; it's okay to have a quiet and calming gathering room if you want it that way, with softer colors or the same colors as the rest of your house—in fact, that's my personal preference. It's also equally okay to make your gathering space more vibrant with a color that suits the way you want to feel in the room.

FABRICS

Unless you live by yourself or are hardly ever home, choose durable, stain-resistant fabrics for your gathering room furniture.

Linen feels nice to the touch, and I love its crisp elegance. However, linen wrinkles and stretches out quickly. Linen lovers, consider slipcovers. Purchase two slipcover sets and always have a clean, fresh sofa while one set is being laundered. Linen blends or a linen-look microfiber tend to be more durable, and these fabrics in tan colors or nubby off-white do a nice job of hiding stains. Before ordering fabric online or through a brick-and-mortar store, get a fabric sample to see the actual color in your home.

Leather holds up quite nicely, and some manufacturers have distressed leather options that take the worry out of getting that first big scuff. And look for outdoor fabrics or even indoor-outdoor furniture, which is made to last and is more likely to hold up to whatever your family can dish out.

ACCENTS AND ACCESSORIES

Even though you now have all the big pieces in place, the bones, if you will, your gathering room still might not have that lived in feel. This is where your accents and accessories come into play by adding color, interest, and drama. Reinforce your focal area with lighting and accessories. Ribbon splashes of color all the way around your room, and change accessories out as often as you want to.

Artwork can be a main or secondary focus for your gathering room. A nice painting balances out a TV or adds to a fireplace. It could be original paintings done by you or a friend, or prints purchased from a gallery or garage sale. Enlarge a favorite photo, frame interesting pieces of fabric, or hang vintage signs, antique sporting equipment, doors, mirrors, or windows. Hang one large piece by itself or collage many smaller pieces closely to make a big statement.

Choose colors that are echoed elsewhere in your room or that contrast with bold black-and-white art.

Add accessories that make you more comfortable, year round, as you relax or nap. Throw blankets and pillows encourage your guests to adjust for their own comfort, especially if your sofa and chairs are deep or your room is a little drafty. Keep comfort in mind for snuggling up during cool evenings outside, too. Seasonally, if you want a new look, it's quick to change out the color, fabric, and weight of your blankets and pillows. Nubby fabrics, wool, and dark tones are luxurious in the winter, and linens in light colors are much more refreshing in the summertime.

ENTRYWAYS INTO YOUR HOME

Your entryway is the transition zone from the outside world into your home, your retreat from it all. From the moment anyone arrives at your home, every aspect should be one of welcome and comfort. This zone extends from the curb all the way to the first few steps inside your front door—at least, as much as you have control over.

The thing to remember is that the entry is for you as much as it is for guests, if not more. A lot more, actually. Who goes in and out of your home more than you do? In order to love coming home, you have to start with the entrance!

You might have an entrance used only by guests, and a different one that you normally use, maybe from the garage or through the laundry room. So-called mud rooms work hard, but that doesn't mean they need to be messy, dark, and ugly. Put as much attention into your family entryway as you would the formal one your guests use, even though the functions are going to be quite different. Often, the family entrance becomes the friends entrance too, and the formal entrance is left to first-time visitors, dinner party attendees, and people who make deliveries or handle repairs.

If you have two entries, two separate design projects might be required. You can prioritize one over the other or do them both at the same time.

START BY SETTING YOUR INTENTION

The entry points into your home should be welcoming and should give clues about the real you. Your entry to your home should set the first impression for your personal style. Think of the formal entryway into your home as the house version of yourself being presentable for work, and the other entryway as the at-home casual version. Everyday, effortless, comfortable, normal. But still you, not anyone else.

THE FAMILY ENTRYWAY

Your family entry can be the T-shirt and jeans version of your formal entryway. It's still comfortable, welcoming, and presentable but more functional. If this is your laundry room, you can choose to hide the washer and dryer with shutters, doors, or draped fabric, or keep them out in plain (but neat) sight. Stash dirty clothes in hampers, and keep detergents and supplies out of view as well. It's as easy for everyone in your family to drop dirty clothes in a hamper as it is to drop them on the floor! The last thing you want to see when you get home from a busy workday is a big pile of dirty laundry.

How far into your home do you bring the mail and your keys? Where do you set your backpack, handbag, or groceries? Sports equipment? Is there a coat closet nearby or do you need to create one? Do you have muddy boots, wet jackets, umbrellas, hats, and gloves to deal with? Do you need a place for pet leashes, food, and toys? Do you take your shoes off before getting very far into your house?

Add cabinetry with a bench and open shoe storage below, hooks for coats and backpacks, and shelving for gloves and hats. Off-the-shelf or custom made by a cabinetmaker, this type of storage system should have a cubby for each member of your family, including your fur babies.

If you have extra room, add a "drop zone" to sort mail and store keys. Place recycling containers and a heavy-duty shredder nearby, so you can shred junk mail without even opening it. Doing these things means that the mess won't make it very far into your house, and you get to eliminate a little bit of clutter before it materializes.

WHAT IS THE FOCUS?

For larger, grander entries, the focus could be a statement table with flowers or a plant. If you have the space, a work of art or something dramatic hanging above an entry table is a nice touch. A secondary focus could be a bench or chair, and a tree. I've seen entryways double as a music room, complete with a grand piano! The key is to let your personality shine right as your front door opens. Let the look and fragrance of your entryway be a cue to the rest of your home.

For a smaller entryway, have at least a mirror so you can take that last glance at yourself before you leave. A mirror can also make the space feel larger.

INSIDER'S TIP: A word of caution about mirrors in entryways . . . actually, mirrors in any area of your home . . . pay attention to what they reflect! It is all-to-common to see the mirror itself but fail to notice what's actually being reflected in it. Be sure your mirror isn't reflecting a toilet from a nearby powder room. I've seen it more times than I can count!

Instead of a mirror, you might prefer to hang something on the wall that adds a more personal touch, and below it, perhaps a small table for your keys and mail.

For the tiniest entries, a narrow hall that leads into the main part of your house, have a mirror, and maybe a basket for your shoes. Keep your small entry clean—no clutter at all. Maybe your laundry area can hold your shoes and hooks for your coats, or a bench and coat rack further in, at your kitchen.

ESTABLISHING YOUR PALETTE, PAINTS, AND FABRICS

Since your entryway is a sneak peek into the rest of your house, your colors and style should tie in closely. You can create an Entryway Vision Board—in fact,

I encourage it—to see to it that your entryway coordinates with adjacent areas and doesn't end up feeling disconnected. However, in an entryway you can amp things up and make the space a bit more grand and important, allowing for a sense of arrival.

ACCENTS

Even the biggest entryways don't have a large number of accents, but the ones they do have should be there on purpose. This is not a place to store leftover objects or items that are no longer important to you. Remember, this space sets the tone for the rest of your home. Keeping accents simple helps frame the primary focus, but you can have fun with what you choose to highlight in your entryway.

Choose art or large mirrors that you love. Position special accessories you want to be sure your guests see. If you opt for a dramatic plant or a dried flower arrangement, be prepared to dust frequently, since dusty (neglected?) is not the tone you want to set. The same goes for wreaths hanging on the outside of your front door.

That being said, entryways are not the best place to show off a collection, loads of small accent pieces, or a full-sized photo of your family. These items tend to look more like clutter than intentionally placed plants or works of art.

AREA RUGS

No matter how large your entry is, provide a good-sized rug to soften the area and act as an inside doormat. It probably shouldn't be expensive, as it will take considerable wear and tear. Scale it to fit the area, but opt for something big enough that you can step twice on each foot to help keep your house clean. Check the height of the pile so that your front door can open and close freely without getting caught on the rug, and be sure to have a sizable doormat outside the front door. Depending on the rules of your building, a welcome mat is a great way to personalize your door in a long hallway. It doesn't need to be printed with the word welcome, but keep in mind that the mat you choose sets the tone for what you want to experience when you and your guests step into your home.

LIGHTING

As in your other rooms, the lighting in your entryway is best if layered. If you have space, a central chandelier, on a dimmer, adds ambiance and sets the tone for the rest of your house. Or maybe your space is better served by wall sconces or lamps on a table. Having more than one light source makes the space feel more interesting. If you have framed art in your entryway, mounting an inexpensive art light above the piece adds a new dimension and lends greater importance to the piece..

Whatever lamp you might have in your entryway, try using an energy-efficient lightbulb in it. Plug this lamp into a timer set to turn it on at a certain time each day. It's comforting to have a light on when you come home, and it can serve a security purpose, too.

WHERE YOU FEAST:
DINING ROOMS AND KITCHENS

Nothing is truly formal in my house. For each place where eating happens, I've set different intentions, but what they have in common is that I want my family and my guests to feel comfortable eating anywhere. Myself included. Messes happen, and that's okay. I don't want to have anything so precious in my house that I have to chase guests away from any spot. And we do live with white in nearly every room.

The key is to use washable fabrics and have stain remover close at hand. If you tackle a spill the moment it happens, you can usually get it out. If you have kids, you probably don't want to be vigilant with stain remover daily, so you might want to opt for a slightly darker tone to your fabrics that will soften the effect of stains.

Another commonality with all the places we eat is that they often serve multiple purposes. Dining tables are also workspaces for food prep, doing crafts, wrapping gifts, playing cards, and much more. Even so, the primary purpose of dining spaces is as a place in which to feast.

START BY SETTING YOUR INTENTION

Since you may eat in several different places throughout your home, set your purpose and intention for each feasting space. Some rooms should be more specific to eating, and it's okay for other rooms to multitask. For example, how do you want your kitchen counter and barstools to function as opposed to your actual dining table? Without an obvious place to eat, a house isn't very inviting. A table surrounded by more chairs than occupants of the home represents generosity and hospitality, and you can make this work in any space, no matter how small!

Think about how you currently use your house, especially your dining room, if you have one. Do you *ever* eat there? Is your family eating in other places, where you'd rather they not? Do you always have to get your kids to clear their homework or crafts from the table before setting it for dinner? How often do you entertain in the dining room . . . really?

Own Your Feasting Space!

No matter if you have a big dining room or a small one, entertain accordingly, and don't apologize for anything about it. Not that your chairs or dishes don't match, that your table isn't big enough, or that your buffet surface is made out of a long folding table. Choose the dining table that works for you and for your space. If your dining room table seats six comfortably, set your intention to have an amazing formal dinner for six. Or even four. But if you want to entertain more guests and your table and chairs won't accommodate a higher number, set your intention for a more casual experience. Present the food buffet style in the kitchen, and use benches for increased seating at that same table. Or have an outdoor space that will seat more people. Or let everyone sit in the family room. The choice is yours, just own it!

WHAT IS THE FOCUS?

The focus of a dining room is generally the table itself, whether it's set for dinner or not, while the rest of the room acts as a frame for the eating functions and the aesthetics. Since feasting requires dishes, glassware, and flatware, not to mention service items, centerpieces, tablecloths, runners, and maybe chair covers in several colors for the seasons, storage is important in any dining area.

After your table, your storage furniture can provide a secondary focus, perhaps a cabinet or armoire, a rolling bar cart, or a buffet with a mirror or artwork over it. Think about furniture that can store your extra dishes, of course, but depending on other activities planned for the room, you might want to consider a shelving unit with baskets for the kids' craft supplies, or drawers to hold your hobby gear.

LAY OUT YOUR FURNITURE

To determine your dining room furniture placement, lay out your furniture on graph paper, large items first. And here's a tip: make a dotted line around the dining table that is three feet away from its edge. That way you will remember to leave enough space for the chairs!

Let's talk about the table itself, and how to choose the right one. It's going to be the largest piece of furniture in the room. Do you want it to be round, square, or rectangle? How large should it be? How many people will be regularly seated there, and what type of seating do you prefer? Benches, armchairs, upholstered chairs, or wooden dining chairs? Which works with the table shape you like? Lots of questions, but I'll help you figure out how to answer

them. First, figure out the table size you need. Then you can keep your eyes out for a table in a style you love.

A round table with a 36-inch diameter takes up less floor space than a 36-inch square table. But, the square table's corners allow for more elbowroom, literally. If you need to occasionally squeeze in more people, think about the table legs. Pedestal or trestle style legs are better for flexible seating, since no one has to straddle a leg.

Your dining room seating should be comfortable and durable. If your room is large, chairs with tall backs will help your dining table feel like a room within a room, for intimate or more private dining experiences. For smaller rooms, choose open back chairs that are a little shorter. This will help make the dining space feel part of the bigger room, not as separate.

Whether you have seat cushions, fabric chair covers, or upholstered chairs is up to you. Padded fabric makes dining chairs more comfortable for feasting that lasts far into the night, but keep fabric care in mind. Removable cushions and chair covers are often washable, and you get to change them out with the season or whenever you feel like it.

Other ideas to consider for your dining room include a coffee station, a cocktail bar, or space for serving and storing wine.

If your dining room is your secondary feasting area, and you need a place to read or enjoy an espresso and conversation with a friend, maybe four lounge chairs around a large round coffee table will be a good alternative to a traditional dining table. Or perhaps a card table and chairs will be perfect for family game nights. Be creative, and remember to suit your needs.

AREA RUGS

You don't have to add an area rug underneath your dining table, but it does help set this area apart for dining, especially if your floors are made of wood, stone, or tile. Use a rug that is large enough to allow the chairs to move out and easily accommodate all four legs on the rug, and smooth enough or with a low pile that lets chairs move freely. A good rule of thumb is to use an area rug that is at least two feet larger than your table on all sides.

LIGHTING

Out of all the rooms in your home that require different levels of lighting and a dimmer switch, your dining room is at the top of the list. Whether sharing a glass of wine or hosting a dinner party, setting the right lighting level is an elemental part of setting the mood.

Choose your chandelier or pendant-style lighting according to your Room Vision Board. This light provides both ambient and accent lighting. In the case of a dining room, you don't need much ambient lighting at all, unless you're doing a deep clean in the evening. Scale the chandelier to your table and your room, so it looks in balance. If your table is really long, consider more than one pendant in a row.

Adding sconces on the wall or a lamp on your buffet table helps with harsh overhead shadows and balances out the light. Put these accent lights on dimmers, too, and be sure to use the same type of lightbulb in all fixtures. Candles on the table, whether electric or real, add a soft glow and a more flattering light. As with every room, having a few layers of lighting adds drama and beauty.

If you don't have a place for an overhead fixture over your table, you can still have dramatic and beautiful light. Some lightweight chandeliers hang from a hook and have a long cord that you can plug directly into a wall outlet. This works really well when you can't install electricity in the ceiling. Or look for a floor lamp that has a high arch and a heavy base. This is a great option for modern décor styles. You can use strands of white lights on a tall tree in the corner or string them across the room if you'd like. Review your Vision Boards for lighting that might work as well in a dining room as in a living room.

WINDOW TREATMENTS

Typically, privacy isn't an issue in a dining space, so window treatments aren't always necessary. However, if you want to add a little more warmth to the room, hanging full-length fabric panels at each side of the window might be all you need. For color, consider what you have in your adjacent rooms. It's rare that a dining room is a completely separate room, isolated all on its own, so you can use the same drapery panels you have in another area, or coordinate them with a tone in your area rug or dining chairs.

ESTABLISHING YOUR PALETTE

A dining room offers a unique opportunity to use some deeper accent colors if it's set off on its own. Or keep it simple and quiet, matching the wall and ceiling colors to adjacent rooms. We walk by our dining room every time we enter our home, so I opt to keep the walls white to seamlessly flow with the rest of our home.

I had a client who . . . painted their dining room jet black with white trim. It was seriously stunning and unexpected. It worked because the room was off on its own, not directly connected to any other room, and it had plenty of light.

FABRICS

Except for your window treatments, table coverings, and possible upholstery on dining chairs, dining rooms include few fabrics. For practicality, choose easy-care tablecloths, placemats, and napkins that will withstand heavy use, but still make choices based on your personal design style. Use themes or colors that you pull from your Vision Boards. Table linens work in a similar way as an accessory item. If you have a shiny table, a matte finish to your tabletop items will look best, and if you have a matte finish on your table, choose fabrics with notable texture or sheen to offer contrast.

For upholstered chairs, leather or outdoor fabrics are highly durable, but the main thing is to have something you can wash easily. My dining room chairs are fully upholstered in white linen, and they've weathered many spills. Many! The key for us has been addressing spills immediately.

WHAT CAN YOU REPURPOSE, AND WHAT SHOULD YOU TOSS?

Is your existing dining table the right size and color? Is your table nice enough? Or perhaps too nice, leaving you afraid to use it without a tablecloth for protection? Are the chairs comfortable and undemanding to move? Do you have a good option for storage?

As you did for your gathering room, take photos of the pieces you are thinking of keeping, and add them to your Dining Room Vision Board. Does a given piece blend in or look out of place? Does it add function? Do you truly love it? Are you hanging onto Grandma's china set only because you have the space? Can you do some decluttering to save yourself from buying new storage furniture? If your chairs are comfortable and your table is the right size, you might be able to give them a new look. You can sand down the wood and spray-paint it. And you can recover a dining chair using a screwdriver, staple gun, foam, and new fabric, or cover it completely with a slipcover.

ACCENTS AND ACCESSORIES

Dining rooms need fewer accents to feel lived in than other rooms, but you can still have some fun with color and scale for interest and drama. The table is the room's primary focus, and you can choose to accessorize it as much or as little as you want. In my opinion, less is more. You could opt for a little bit of greenery in the center of the table, and when you're entertaining, add a few candles. Let the food and wine be the hero on your dining table.

THE KITCHEN IS THE HEART OF YOUR HOME

In your home, which room is the busiest? Where do your party guests come find you and linger? Where the food is, where the warming fires for cooking are—the center of your home, socially and functionally. Food is a gift; it is both nutrition and pleasure, as well as something we celebrate.

There is wisdom in the adage that the way to a person's heart is through their stomach!

Most people think about kitchen improvements only as an expensive remodeling project or the replacement of appliances. Not so! You can make your kitchen work more efficiently and be more social without ripping apart the walls. Set your intentions as strongly for the kitchen as you would any other room in your house.

I had a client who . . . loved her new house but hated her gigantic kitchen. While a major remodel isn't really the point of this book, this is a fun story about how big doesn't always mean better. This kitchen had a colossal granite island that was bigger than a king-sized bed. It had acres of counter space, restaurant-sized appliances, and two huge walk-in pantries. Although she was an avid cook who enjoyed throwing elaborate dinner parties, it wasn't until she moved in and put groceries away for the first time that she discovered how much walking she was going to have to do to get around her enormous kitchen. Getting milk for her morning coffee felt like a major chore.

The kitchen had the classic work triangle of sink-refrigerator-range, but because everything was so big, the appliances were far away from each other. She called me, and with a few adjustments and converting the one big island into two, we created two work triangles. One was for prep and cooking, anchored by the range, refrigerator, and a small prep sink. A completely separate work triangle facilitated cleanup, with a full-sized sink and two dishwashers. All of a sudden, her big kitchen became two smaller but much more functional complementary spaces. She even had space for a charming wine storage and wet bar area, so her guests could access drinks and socialize without walking deep into the kitchen.

START BY SETTING YOUR INTENTION

Besides the obvious requirements for cooking, cleaning, and storage, let's consider how you can make your *now* kitchen the best it can be by setting your intention for your ultimate dream kitchen. Dig out or create your Kitchen Vision Board. What does your kitchen need to do for you? Is your dream kitchen a magnificent showplace? What color are the counters, the cabinets, and the walls? What do you really need? Is your kitchen your main feasting area? Does your dream include a large farmhouse worktable dusty with flour for kneading bread or making pies? Shelves galore and a big pantry for your canning habit and Costco runs? Do you envision a cozy bistro area or nook in which you and your partner can enjoy a glass of wine? A crafts area for your kids? How about a feeding and pet-care center for the furriest members of your family?

These intentions can help you dedicate existing seating areas to be flexible and multipurpose, or more specific if that suits you better. For example, if you love the farm table idea but don't have enough space, perhaps you can replace the top to your island with wood planks, and find new or old chairs or stools in the right style. Or add shelves to store your wine collection and barware.

WHAT IS THE FOCUS?

The main function of your kitchen should be the preparation of food and drink. The primary focus is the warmest part, the fire, if you will—where you cook! The stove, or range, represents fire. In any kitchen, large or small, emphasize this area by giving the range plenty of space, contrasting the finish of the appliances for drama rather than working to make the cooktop or vent hood blend into the surrounding cabinetry.

If you're planning a new kitchen from scratch, make the range the focal point by centering it on a wall, wherever it makes sense, most likely the longest wall or the one you see first when walking into the room. Even if your apartment's kitchen is on the blah side, you can achieve this effect by adding temporary accents to the backsplash, like hanging heatproof art or maybe vintage dinner plates and utensils above the stove (ask a contractor for ideas on how to safely hang items here). You can also suspend a pot rack or change the lighting. Attaching temporary wall coverings to some of the cabinetry could be a fun and landlord-friendly alternative to painting.

Your eating area is an inviting secondary focus, with elements you can bring with you if a move is in your future. Plan to have at least barstools or chairs, and if you have the space, possibly a table. If your stove area is boring and you can't do anything about it yet, bump up the impact of your feasting area, making the table, counter, kitchen island, or whatever you have be the primary focus. Even if you eat at the kitchen counter, choose dramatic lighting and interesting seating, table settings, tablecloths or runners, and so forth, to create a warm, inviting part of your kitchen.

Another secondary focal feature could be your beverage center: be it wine, cocktails, or coffee. Choose a charming vintage table, a freestanding armoire that opens up and functions as liquor or glassware storage, or a shorter buffet. Such storage pieces can also stand in as a pantry or serving area. Bar carts—beverage centers on wheels—can be rolled around when you entertain.

LAY OUT YOUR FURNITURE

Your kitchen is a workspace, not the best place in your home for an abundance of furniture. Options include a dining table, chairs or stools, and, if you don't have an island, accent tables, carts, or cabinets. Take notes from your feasting room, though you may not even need to draw up this space. Whatever furniture you choose, allow plenty of room to move around it. At a minimum, allow at least 36 inches between furniture and cabinetry, though 48 inches would be better. You might require more space if you need to back up a chair or have more than one person working in the kitchen at the same time. To help you figure out what the result will be if you are considering a table, outline the size in removable masking tape you'd use for painting, or stacking cardboard boxes into the right size and height. Live with that for a day or two to see what you think.

AREA RUGS

Unless your kitchen is gigantic, you probably don't have space for an area rug. If you do, consider a durable indoor-outdoor rug that will hold up to the inevitable dirt, stains, crumbs, and heavy traffic. A mat or rug by the sink or range makes sense if you have back problems or discomfort while standing, but make sure it is easy to keep clean and dry. If you let your personality shine through a little bit, it may even become the element that ties in all the other accents in your kitchen. Look to your Kitchen Vision Board for color clues and choose your floor mat or rug with intention. As for any other room in your home, your kitchen should be grounded by some of the colors you see at your mid level and eye level.

LIGHTING

Your kitchen is a workspace, so the level of ambient lighting is important. You need not feel stuck with whatever you already have, since there are clever, easy ways to add extra lighting. Bring light to any dark areas in your kitchen so you're not working in your own shadow. Additional lighting at the stove, prep areas, and sink will help make for a friendlier and more appealing workspace. Some of your lighting can be decorative as well as functional, including special pendant lights over the sink and dining areas. Lamps can work well on counters for extra task lighting, though keep anything with an electrical cord far away from the sink and stove. Battery-operated stick-on lights can be placed underneath your upper cabinets to illuminate countertops. I've installed these in many clients' rental homes, where it would have been impractical to invest in rewiring. Space these puck-shaped lights evenly, and group them fairly close together to avoid an odd spotlight effect.

WINDOW TREATMENTS

Matching your kitchen window treatments with the other social areas of your house makes sense, as long as they are no trouble to keep clean. Depending on the level of privacy you need, maybe you won't even need window treatments. Slatted blinds are a helpful option if your sink area faces a window, and the rising or setting sun causes glare.

ESTABLISHING YOUR PALETTE

Kitchen colors can be lively, but the materials need to be durable, especially for counters, cabinets, and flooring. Pull ideas from your Kitchen Vision Board for your wall and cabinet colors, though plan out this step if your existing colors are quite different and would exceed the boundaries of a DIY project. If you need to replace counters or flooring, for example, ask a contractor how extensive the project might be, and then plan ahead using your budget and Projects List.

In the meantime, neutralize colors you don't care for with paint (ask at the paint store about the proper preparation and suitability) or temporary wallpaper. You can even hide ugly accent tiles by hanging your children's artwork.

FABRICS

Think low-maintenance for all your tablecloths, runners, placemats, napkins, and fabric window treatments. Dishtowels, aprons, and so forth can be of any suitable fabric, as long as they're washable. Having a big supply of dishtowels will likely mean you always have a clean one on hand.

PAINT

Painting the walls will quickly freshen up your kitchen. Or maybe all your walls need is a good cleaning! Painting or refinishing your cabinets is a much larger project. Select your colors from your Vision Board to tie in with the rest of your home. For your cabinets, choose a semigloss finish or enamel paint for extra durability and easy cleaning. For practicality, kitchen walls should have a satin finish, but if you don't cook (or need to deep clean) often, the walls could be in an eggshell finish. If you have tall ceilings that blend right into the rest of the home, you can get away with a flat finish for the paint, but know that the finish won't wash well.

You may have to reuse most everything in your kitchen if you're not going to remodel. And that's fine; it happens to most of us. Few can afford to, or even want to, rip out a perfectly good kitchen and start over from scratch every time we move or change our mind about décor style.

Fix anything that is broken, looks worn out, or is a color that you don't love. Minor annoyances—having a couple of broken cabinet door hinges, a noisy garbage disposal unit, or a sink that is too small—can make you want a whole new kitchen. Replace items that don't feel good in your hand. The door and drawer handles? The faucet? Adding or replacing an ugly backsplash can be an easy fix, especially if you don't need to tear out the old backsplash. If you need new counters and backsplash, talk with a few contractors first to understand what might be involved.

INSIDER'S TIP: Be ultra cautious when buying vintage kitchen or bathroom cabinets or any charming old furniture to reuse or refurbish! Same goes for the existing cabinetry in your house, if you want to refinish or paint it. Old cabinets may have lead paint. Buy a test kit at a hardware store before sanding or scraping anything you aren't sure about. Have your treasures professionally stripped offsite to keep the dust out of your lungs and your home.

What should you toss? Clutter! Your kitchen will work much better if it's clutter free. Without building more shelves or adding onto your house, this will magically give you more storage and counter space. Make a game out of editing the contents of the drawers and cabinets, one at a time. Get rid of duplicates: do you really use three sets of measuring spoons or four wine bottle openers? Keep only your favorites. Recycling is a great idea, but what are you saving hundreds of twisty bread ties and rubber bands for? Assign one small clear jar or container for each type of item: twist ties, rubber bands, matches, spare batteries, flashlight bulbs, and so on, and get rid of whatever doesn't fit. Same thing with recycled jam jars, containers for your leftovers, plastic bags for dog walks, and water bottles. Dedicate one drawer or shelf for each, as needed. Don't even bother to save more. Trust me, you won't use them anytime soon! And store the turkey roaster and other items you use once or twice a year someplace else.

A clean kitchen is a healthy kitchen. Unpleasant smells in the kitchen affect your entire home. Maybe it's time for a new garbage can? Consider a small one, so you have to take the trash out more often. Using compostable bags as liners will keep things cleaner for longer, too. If you have pets, a can with a lid makes sense, but lids can be annoying if you have to throw away something big. And, lids are one more thing to keep clean.

Use the vent hood while you're cooking. Consider replacing the exhaust fan if it's ineffectual or so noisy that you don't want to use it. Keeping your vent hood filter clean can cut down on lingering odors. Declare a "filter cleaning hour" and schedule it on your Projects List. It shouldn't take all day. Research online a week or so in advance, though, in case you need to buy filters.

Find, remove, wash, or replace the filter in your dishwasher, too, as this can be a place where odors hang around. I'm sure you can find a YouTube video that will show you how to replace a filter in almost any dishwasher. While you're at it, replace the filters for your refrigerator's water and ice dispensers; it's literally refreshing when the water comes out faster and fresher!

I had a client who . . . saved thousands of dollars by avoiding remodeling. She loved the original 1950s kitchen in her ranch house, but the sink was too shallow for her big pots and pans, which wouldn't fit under the faucet. To her, this made her

entire kitchen feel cramped. The sink was part of a stainless steel drain board and metal cabinet that the tile counter was designed around, so it would be a big, expensive deal to replace and keep the original feel. Instead, she found a tall arched faucet with a pull-out sprayer that instantly created more room for her pots!

ACCENTS AND ACCESSORIES

Even though there is so much activity in a kitchen, there is always room for artwork, interesting pieces of wood, vintage signs, treasures, wine bottles, beautiful pots and pans, or special countertop appliances, such as an Italian espresso maker. Anything that has something to do with food and drink—even the growing of food—makes sense to display in your kitchen. If you love it, make space for it as an accent, especially if you can hang it on the wall some-place. But remember that even your favorite accessories can quickly overrun your countertop, so unless you use the item daily, find a better place for it.

INSIDER'S TIP: The soffit area between the top of your upper cabinets and the ceiling, is not real storage space! It's hard to reach, and whatever is up there quickly gets dusty. Choose a few dishwasher-safe items as accents for that space—oversized glass jars, bottles, pitchers, vases, and similar items. Faux plants and baskets are great as temporary display, but because they're hard to clean, why bother.

11

Personal Spaces:
From Bedrooms
to Bathrooms

*Your sacred space is where you find yourself
over and over again.*

Joseph Campbell

While gathering rooms and feasting areas are the social, active areas of your home, the bedrooms and bathrooms are usually private, for you, your family, and perhaps for overnight guests. Generally, these rooms are a step or two away from social areas, down a hall, separated for quiet and peacefulness. Not all family members sleep at the same time, so the remote location helps reduce noise from TVs, conversation, the kitchen, and activity late into the night or early the next day. While the aroma of freshly brewed coffee is pleasant early in the morning, the whining coffee grinder . . . not so much!

When you do entertain, your bedroom and personal bathroom are universally recognized as *your* private space. Most people respect a closed door, and that's rarely questioned. However, the flip side to this privacy is that we often let bedrooms and bathrooms turn into catchall rooms. Guest rooms, in particular, might be like a drawer where you shove unfolded clothes, intending to clean up someday. Also, since they're for our own use, we rarely show off the bedrooms. Unlike a flashy new kitchen or stunning new sectional, our tendency is to give bedrooms the lowest priority in our home. It's sometimes hard to spend money on ourselves, especially for a private room nobody else sees.

You deserve a room that supports your soul, and it's not a waste of time, attention, and money to create a space you love. A room for yourself is a haven away from it all, a private retreat where you can celebrate the start and the end to your day, and any other time in between. Everyone in your family deserves this. It's worth the effort!

THE MASTER BEDROOM

Your bedroom is the most personal room in your house, the most intimate, the most private. Even if your bedroom is small or you don't have extra money at the moment, you can make your bedroom comfortable, inviting, and personal, as well as a luxurious place to share with your partner.

After all, you spend a third of your whole life in your bedroom—ideally sleeping six to eight hours every day, in addition to the time you spend dressing or relaxing. Quality sleep is one of the best ways to improve your life, and making your own bedroom a retreat from the pressures of daily life isn't all that difficult or expensive.

Unfortunately, it's tempting to add function to your bedroom because you might have the space. Seeing your exercise equipment or a desk while you are wrapping up your evening might remind you of how busy your day was. Thinking about your unfinished to-do list isn't the best way to relax!

Reducing your bedroom's function to sleep, relaxation, and romance, even if you have space for more, will help create an environment for quality sleep and a healthier, more loving lifestyle.

START BY SETTING YOUR INTENTION

For most rooms in your house, there are typical intentions that make sense. Beyond those, add your own intentions that will personalize your home. Your bedroom, however, is the one room that I will be more specific and suggest you set your intention for quality sleep and tranquility. *My* intention for *your* bedroom is that in it you feel calm, restful, and at peace. I hope you'll agree!

I'm always inspired when I travel, and I have stayed in hotels all over the world. A lot of them! The thing I love best about spending time in a well-designed hotel room is that there is little stress. It reminds me of being on vacation, far removed from everyday life and anxieties, and with no chores. Everything is clean, neat, and organized, and I'm not the one to clean it!

When my husband and I moved into our home together, I set up our bedroom to feel calm, restful, and luxurious, like a nice hotel room. We make a real effort to keep it clean and clutter free. Because I don't need to worry about the state of our bedroom, it's a relaxing and romantic place to spend time with my husband. We sleep better, too, with the stresses of our daily life stacked up outside, in some other room.

What are your intentions for your private space, besides being a great place for quality sleep and relaxation—one that promotes a sense of calm and tranquility? What other activities happen in your bedroom now? Aside from sleep, romance, relaxation, dressing, and storing your clothes, seriously consider moving other activities to another place in your home.

WHAT IS THE FOCUS?

Your bed should be the primary focal point in your bedroom. If you have high ceilings, a bed with a canopy or a tall four-poster works nicely to create a cozy space within the space. A headboard of some sort will anchor the bed visually, emphasizing this focal point. It will also help create an inviting sleeping zone. If you don't want to buy a whole bed, attach a salvaged door or artful pieces of wood, paint a rectangle, or place a bookcase or room-dividing screen or panel at the head of your bed.

Have the mattress elevated off the floor. My mom made five-sided boxes out of wood that supported our childhood mattresses off the floor. This will help your mattress breathe, reducing allergens, mold, and mildew. However, whatever you use to lift your mattress off the floor, it should provide a stable and quiet base. That makes all the difference to a good night's sleep.

Invest in the softest bedding you can afford. Having soft textures against your skin not only feels good, it also helps you sleep better. And by all means make your bed every single morning! Right when you get out of it.

I like to keep beds simple: sheets, maybe a blanket and a duvet or coverlet. For the bed as a decorative element, less is more. Sleeping pillows should stack right behind shams for no-fuss access. The shams can be rectangular shaped or square, also known as Euro shams, depending on the shape you prefer. Two is all you need. If desired, pop on a couple accent pillows in colors you love that tie the other decorative elements of your room together. For temperature variation, you can also add a folded coverlet or oversized throw blanket at the foot of the bed. My quilted coverlet doubles as a dog-proofing element. Before leaving for the office in the morning, I pull the coverlet to the top to keep the bed free from dog prints. Then when I get home, my freshly made bed is underneath.

LAY OUT YOUR FURNITURE

Before moving anything physically, lay out your furniture on graph paper, large items first. Place the bed against the longest wall in the room, hopefully with plenty of space on both sides, but ideally not against a window or facing the door. What size bed? Just big enough! If your room is tiny and you live on your own, perhaps a full or twin bed will work out nicely, so you have more space to move around and not feel cramped. If you have more space, don't feel you have to have a big bed unless you really want one. If you have a regular sleeping partner, many people prefer at least a queen-sized bed. If you have a large room, a king-sized bed will look better because the scale will match your space. My husband is six feet four so we opt for a California King, which is a little longer and less wide than a regular king bed.

Most people need to store clothing and dress in their bedrooms because they don't have separate dressing rooms or large closets. Closets in older homes are rarely adequate even if they are walk-in closets, and adding a dresser or an armoire helps keep clothing organized. Store only the clothes you actually wear; get rid of the rest.

Having someplace other than your bed to sit down is a luxury, as long as you don't stack it with laundry! If you have the space, a reading chair or two, a small table, and a lamp offer a nice place to unwind at the end of the day. Or try a large bench, a chaise, or a small sofa at the foot of the bed.

I don't usually recommend a TV or any electronics in your bedroom, but I admit we have one in ours. The ideal scenario if you have a TV in your bedroom is to hide the TV and equipment when you're not watching it. An armoire can be a beautiful counterpoint to your bed, and it does a great job of hiding things. If you have your TV mounted on the wall, cover any glowing power lights. A small piece of black electrical tape works wonders. Exposed, those lights are not conducive to a good sleep environment, as they can mimic daylight and disrupt sleep.

ADD YOUR ACCENT FURNITURE

Don't forget the nightstands! Have one for each sleeper as a place for a lamp, book, glass of water or cup of tea, and maybe a notepad for nighttime thoughts. But not your cellphone . . . try to eliminate electronics from your bedroom. I understand that many people use their phone as an alarm clock, and if you do, I recommend placing it in the hallway or in the bathroom, with the ringer on loud. If you must have your phone in your bedroom, consider taking advantage of its do-not-disturb settings. You might also try placing your phone inside a folded towel to muffle vibrations that might otherwise wake you up.

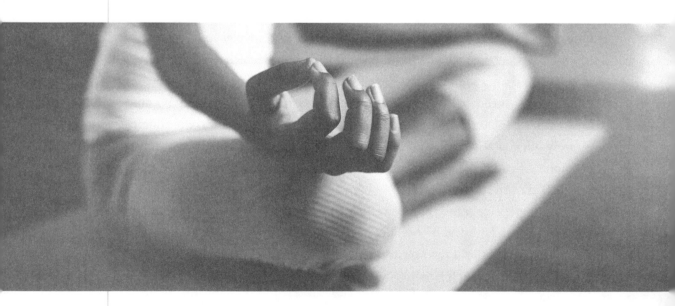

Nightstands don't have to match each other but should relate, with similar wood tones or shapes. They can be tables or even small dressers if you need the storage space.

AREA RUGS

An area rug, even if you already have carpet, adds color and interest to a bedroom. You can be creative with placement and size, though if you have noncarpeted flooring, at a minimum, place a small rug on each side of the bed so you have a warm place to stand. A large rug arranged symmetrically under the bed helps reinforce the bed as a focal point, or you could angle, or even layer rugs for greater interest and drama.

A good rule of thumb when determining size: queen beds do best with an eight by ten-foot rug and king beds typically need a nine by twelve or larger.

LIGHTING

Downward light from recessed can fixtures or a chandelier provides general lighting in the bedroom, but it is not flattering to anyone. For a romantic feeling, use table or floor lamps, and have dimmers on every light source in the bedroom so you can adjust their brightness at night.

WINDOW TREATMENTS

Bedrooms call for privacy. Even if you don't have close neighbors, window treatments will help you feel safer and more comfortable in your bedroom. In addition, you will need to control external light more in your bedroom than any other room in your home, especially if you or your sleeping partner work different hours or you have bright street lighting outside.

For bedrooms, in particular, my clients have often preferred to go with softer choices, such as translucent sheers for daytime, layered with linen drapery panels. You can back the drapery panels with a blackout liner to have total darkness and privacy anytime you need it. As in any room, horizontal blinds also offer a good balance between light control and privacy. Turning blind slats downward will protect your privacy while allowing daylight to filter into your room.

ESTABLISHING YOUR PALETTE

Bedrooms with a soft, light color palette feel calm and tranquil, which is perfect for sleep and relaxation. Right now my entire house, including my bedroom, is painted a soft white, and my accents are charcoal and grays. Other colors that work well for bedroom walls or accents are ivory, buttercream, off-whites, or pale tones of gray, lavender, blue, sage, or tan. Look at your Room Vision Board, and pull out the calmest colors for your walls.

But that doesn't mean calm has to be boring. You can go bolder with accent colors if you want to, especially for your bedding. Navy blue, deep burgundy reds, multiple shades of tan or gray give you interest and drama without going too bold.

FABRICS

All your bedroom fabrics, especially your bedding, should be soft and luxurious. This is not the place to experiment with a variety of different textures, like you might in your gathering room. For chairs and accents, try soft linens and velvets.

For your bedding, choose whatever feels softest to you. I prefer something that doesn't require ironing, for easy care, plus it always looks great. Use color tones that support the intention of how you want your room to feel and function. Take cues directly from your Master Bedroom Vision Board.

ACCENTS AND ACCESSORIES

You don't need a great deal of furniture or accents for your bedroom. In fact, keeping your bedroom sparse will make it feel calm, relaxing, airy, and free of dust. If you want to personalize your master bedroom beyond the bedding and furniture items, sparingly use romantic and tranquil accents, such as candles or photos from happy times, possibly representing you and your sweetie. If you have space for art, go for soft colors that add interest without being overwhelming or overstimulating.

INSIDER'S TIP: Ferns on the nightstands add a softening effect and Japanese royal ferns and Boston ferns are known to help purify the air. Some plant experts even claim plants like lavender and jasmine help you sleep better.

WHAT CAN YOU REPURPOSE, AND WHAT SHOULD YOU TOSS?

Bedrooms, especially the master bedroom, are often low on people's priority list. Sometimes it's preferable to put money into the more visible parts of the house, such as the kitchen, or a new sofa and updated TV for a gathering space. But because we spend so much time in bed, your mattress, pillows, and bedding should be a huge priority. A good-quality, comfortable bed—the best you can afford—is something you deserve to have.

We often take our mattress and pillows for granted, and then wonder why we wake up stiff or congested, with swollen eyes. Beds wear out quicker than you think they do. If your mattress is more than seven years old, consider replacing it. If it is more than ten years old or is a hand-me-down of dubious age, replace it! If your pillows are more than two years old, they, too, should be replaced.

Your other bedroom furniture can be replaced as you need or want to, according to your Master Bedroom Vision Board. Painting or refinishing nightstands, dressers, beds, and other bedroom furniture may allow you to personalize your look and be creative while staying within your budget

KIDS' BEDROOMS

You don't need much to make a kid's room work. Young kids, especially, don't have high expectations and are happy with quite simple surroundings. Working as an interior designer, in a multitude of family homes for years, I noticed that as kids grow older, right around age five, they'll start to want to express themselves through their own rooms. The age range varies, but when they start to voice their opinion on their room, let them help! Having control over their bedroom environment teaches them valuable lessons in life. When it's time to make decisions, narrow the options to two or three that you approve of, and let your child choose among them.

Kids also need a calm and tranquil place to sleep and relax. The same ideas that make your bedroom a haven, work for your kids' rooms, too. That means try not to have electronics in the bedroom, including TVs, games, computers, or cell phones. But their color palette can be a little bolder than what you might want in your own room.

I recommend a place for homework outside the bedroom, if you have the space. As intrusive as a home office would be in your bedroom, a desk could be as distracting for your kids. Use your judgment. And see if you can keep only a few toys in the bedroom. Toys and books can be a major distraction at bedtime. If you have the space, create the main play area outside the bedroom, perhaps in the family room or a separate playroom.

The essentials for your child's room include a bed, a comfy reading chair for yourself or the child, a nightstand, a lamp, clothing storage, and a shelf to hold some books and a few toys. Floor pillows that can stack and be turned into forts are fun, as are beanbag chairs and other flexible furniture.

Keep toys and clothing organized with bins, boxes, and low shelves. Use bins small enough that they don't get heavy, and don't stack items too high on a single shelf. Invariably, your child will want whatever is buried the deepest.

Unless it is part of a décor theme, keep sporting equipment out of the bedroom, if possible; it too often clutters the space. A garage, laundry room, or another central area might make more sense—especially if the athletic gear gets smelly!

START BY SETTING YOUR INTENTION

What intentions do you and your child have for their room, besides being a great place for quality sleep, relaxation, getting dressed, and a little bit of playtime?

If your children are involved in setting the intention and making the decisions, they are more likely to take pride in and ownership of their space. They might even keep it cleaner! A clean, calm room with a nicely made bed will help your kids sleep better. And thus, so will you.

Have kids create their own Room Vision Board. It's so much fun to see what a child creates for their own room! It's not only an enjoyable project but it can also translate into all aspects of their life. Early on, teach them the skills needed to create a (life-enhancing) Vision Board.

WHAT IS THE FOCUS?

Like in your master bedroom, the bed is the focus. For kids, though, it can sometimes be the open floor space.

LAY OUT YOUR FURNITURE

Lay out the furniture on graph paper, large items first. Let your child color things in and move the pieces around. While you typically wouldn't put your bed lengthwise against a wall, it is okay to position a child's bed that way. A child's room tends to be smaller, and this gives more space. Also, kids' rooms usually have twin beds, which don't need to be accessed from both sides to make the bed each morning.

Bunk beds and trundle beds are great savers if your kids are sharing a room, or for when a friend sleeps over. Storage furniture for clothing and toys can also be pushed up against the walls.

ADD YOUR ACCENT FURNITURE

Accent furniture for a kid's room can be fun, flexible, and soft. Floor pillows are comfortable chairs, spare mattresses, forts, and so much more. Accessories are likely to be toys and books. And what kid doesn't like to see his or her own name in writing? You can use stencils, paint, or metal letters, which add a fun touch. Vintage sporting equipment or trophies and ribbons can also be used as art for the walls.

AREA RUGS

For a kid's room, an area rug can function as a giant play mat. Even if there isn't something literal in the design, such as a racetrack or village with streets, your child's imagination is boundless. Pick a bold rug with a fun design. Use a large area rug if you don't have carpet, as your kiddo will be spending time playing on it. Stick to a rug with a low pile; it's no fun looking for small toys or parts in a thick, fluffy shag. For an extra plush feel, use a nice rug pad beneath the rug.

LIGHTING

As in any bedroom, lighting scheme and dimmers are worth having in a kid's room, especially as bedtime approaches. A fun lamp can be used for reading, and with an ultra-low setting it can also be used as a nightlight.

WINDOW TREATMENTS

Keep the window treatments fairly inexpensive, as they will probably be damaged at some point. Maybe use a roller shade or decorative panels that coordinate with their décor. And make triple sure your window treatments, especially in your child's room, have no cords of any type. The risk of choking is real! Also, keep the bed—and other furniture that kids can climb—away from your windows.

ESTABLISHING YOUR PALETTE

Kids' rooms can be bolder than rooms for adults. Vibrant colors and high contrast are interesting and invigorating, and that is good until it comes time for bed. Bright yellow, for example, could be agitating to some people. And you still want to enjoy going in there.

If red and yellow are your child's favorite colors, choose accents in those colors, not the walls. Or consider softer versions, perhaps a darker red and tan.

Popular adult bedroom colors—ivory, whites, or pale tones of gray, lavender, blue, sage, or tan—work great for kids, but the accents should be more fun. Look at their Room Vision Board and pull out the calmest of their bright colors, get some swatches that you like, and let your kid make the final selection.

FABRICS

From my bed-making days as a housekeeper, I typically saw scratchy bedding for the kids, while the adults got the soft stuff. Kids need to sleep well, and the same sleeping principles apply for kids as for adults. Choose the bedding that feels softest, and confirm that is machine washable for easy care.

Stay away from embellished pillows and anything with super nubby textures, buttons, bows, sequins, or anything that can be swallowed. Instead use printed patterns to up the fun factor in their bedding.

PAINT

For a kid's room, practicality rules. Opt for a paint finish that is a little easier to clean, including the ceiling! Step up to satin finish for the walls and eggshell or satin for the ceiling.

WHAT CAN YOU REPURPOSE, AND WHAT SHOULD YOU TOSS?

Hand-me-downs are great for a kid's room, as long as they are safe and haven't been recalled. Keep antiques and vintage finds, even old toys, out of your child's reach; the paint might contain lead or other toxins.

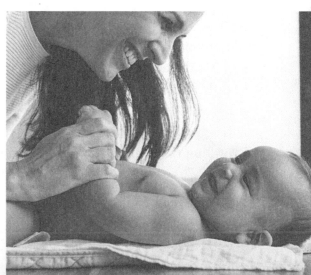

Kids need a comfortable, clean mattress. They might not complain, but they will sleep much better on a suitable mattress. Be sure to use a moisture-resistant (or even waterproof) mattress protector.

NURSERIES

Nurseries are bedrooms for infants and toddlers up to the age of two or three. Nurseries function differently than rooms for older kids. Newborns don't need much room to move around, but they do need a safe place to sleep. And what could be more fun than creating a Room Vision Board for a nursery! This is the one stage in your child's life where you get to call all the shots, so take full advantage of it and have the nursery reflect your personal style 100 percent.

Nurseries need extra furniture to help adults keep babies comfortable. Basic items include: changing table, crib, bassinet, hamper, and a comfy glider or armchair and ottoman. A closet or an armoire may be needed to store clothes. Just like the bed is the hero in your room, let the crib be the hero in your baby's nursery. Review your Vision Board. The crib can be modern or more traditional, and in any color you like, but triple-check that it and any bedding or other additions to the crib meet with all the latest safety standards.

Color schemes in nurseries can and should be more stimulating than in your bedroom.[17] Babies' brains develop in part through their vision, and visual stimulus is fundamental. Bright colors, high contrast, and bold geometric shapes on the walls and closer to their cribs give babies fun things to focus on, both far and near. Zebra stripes and huge graphic patterns would probably be the ideal nursery wallpaper if you could stand it. You and I get plenty of stimuli in our daily life; babies don't have much of an outside life and thus depend on their immediate surroundings for variety.[18]

We are not really sure how colors affect babies or how they even see color, but we know more about how colors affect adults. We also know that babies pick up on how we feel, so select colors that work for you.

Use several light sources in the nursery for maximum flexibility. Dimmers make it easy to check on your baby without waking him or her up, or to avoid tripping on a toy in the dark. Lamps make nice touches, but security first! Make sure cords are completely inaccessible to a baby or toddler.

When purchasing furniture especially dressers or armoires, make sure they are secured to the wall, so your child can't accidentally pull them over on themselves as they learn to walk and climb. Also try to invest in pieces that can grow with your child. Most dressers and armoires, if well made, can make it from babyhood to the teenage years by repainting or refinishing, or changing the hardware.

GUEST ROOMS

An ideal guest room should provide the comforts of home while being clean, warm, and inviting, but it doesn't need to be fancy. Test your guest room personally—pack a bag and pretend you're a guest. You'll notice right away if anything needs changing or if you forgot to add something.

A sense of privacy is more important than the ultimate bed or an exquisitely decorated room. A closed door goes a long way toward making everyone feel more comfortable. But if you have only a corner of an office or hobby room to dedicate to guests, that's okay, too. Try not to share the space with your guests while they're visiting, though. Plan accordingly if you work from home.

If you have a room-dividing screen, place it in front of your desk or shelves to hide the rest of the office furniture. Center the bed on the screen, and the room will be neatly divided into guest space and office space.

START BY SETTING YOUR INTENTION

If you have a dedicated guest bedroom, take notes from the best hotel rooms you've ever been in. If you have a semi-dedicated guest room, set your intentions with the appropriate priorities according to your needs and the comfort of your guests.

It's okay to set your own parameters as well as your own personal intention for your guest room. For example, if you enjoy short-term guests, set your intention for the space to be the best guest bedroom they'll ever experience . . . for three days. Or overnight. Whatever works for you. Intentions are a little like affirming your own boundaries, and setting them makes it easier to enforce them.

WHAT IS THE FOCUS?

If this is a dedicated guest room, the bed should be the primary focal point, as in your master bedroom. If your guest space shares a room with some other function, such as your home office or a hobby room, make the bed be the temporary focus when you have guests.

A big difference between a dedicated guest bedroom and your master bedroom would be that while I don't recommend a small desk in your own bedroom, it's a nice touch in a guest bedroom. Just as you would like to have all your possessions, including your cell phone, laptop, and other electronics, handy in a hotel room, your guests will want their electronics close at hand, too.

LAY OUT YOUR FURNITURE

If you have a dedicated guest room, lay out your furniture on graph paper, large items first, as you would for your master bedroom. Consider having two twin beds, which is a flexible option that works for a variety of guests, especially if you have more than one guest room.

Add a small desk and task chair. The desk can double as a nightstand. And, if you want to provide a TV, you don't need to hide it; make it accessible and easy to use. The guest room is not the place to show off complicated electronic systems. This leads to your guests feeling uncomfortable for having to interrupt you for instructions on how to use the TV, or letting it go unused altogether.

Reserve some clothes hanging space in a closet for your guests, and maybe a drawer or two in a dresser. At a minimum, provide a coat rack with empty hangers if you have no closet.

ADD YOUR ACCENT FURNITURE

Your guests will need nightstands. Place one on each side of the bed, or perhaps one between two twin beds if you're short on space. Accordingly, provide a lamp. Water bottles on the nightstands are a nice touch, with maybe a plant and a tissue box, but that's about it. Guest bedroom nightstands are not the place to highlight your treasured accessories or family photos.

Adding a mirror someplace in the room brightens and eases morning routines, especially if the bathroom is shared with your family. This could be a full-length mirror or a decorative wall-mounted one.

AREA RUGS, LIGHTING, COLOR PALETTE, WINDOW TREATMENTS, FABRICS, AND ACCENTS

Consider an area rug, lighting, your color palette, window treatments, fabric selections, and accents as you would for your master bedroom, though you can select different colors according to your intentions. For all the same reasons you would in any other room in your home, you should create a Vision Board for your guest room.

Guest rooms sometimes seem to collect all the furniture you have but don't really love and can't figure out where else to put it. You want to love coming

home to every area of your house. If you know this room has become a catchall for what should have been put in the giveaway pile, it will be difficult to feel like smiling inside each time you walk past the room.

Guest-room fabrics should be easy-care and, as a safeguard, hypoallergenic. Have extra blankets on hand for variations in temperature and comfort. Extra bed pillows are often greatly appreciated, too.

Even though flowers can be a nice welcoming touch, some people are sensitive to perfumes and fragrances, so opt for a plant instead. Pay attention to this in hair products, soaps, and even facial tissue. Go for low fragrance in your guest rooms.

WHAT CAN YOU REPURPOSE, AND WHAT SHOULD YOU TOSS?

When you replace furniture in your master bedroom or even your kids' rooms (provided it isn't Disney themed or too juvenile), keep in mind that you might be able to repurpose it in your guest room. Paint or refinish the furniture as needed and in keeping with your Guest Room Vision Board and your color palette. This will help your guest room look intentional, instead of looking like a collection of leftovers.

If your master-bedroom's bed pillows are fairly new and you simply want a different kind for yourself, then feel free to repurpose them in your guest room. Otherwise, toss them. You shouldn't hold on to bed pillows for longer than three years, anyway. Provide two sleeping pillows per side of your guest bed; one can be a softer fill and one medium density, and consider hypoallergenic content and coverings. Decorative pillows add a nice pop of color and style and give the bed a more inviting feel.

You have more leeway with the mattress. In fact, if you need a mattress for a guest room, it could motivate you to replace your master-bedroom mattress a little early. Guest bedrooms are not as regularly used as your primary room, so be content to buy the nicest mattress that fits into your budget.

When space is at a premium, one option is a Murphy bed that pulls down out of cabinetry. Sleeper sofas are another possibility. They have come a long way recently, but they still usually make better sofas than beds.

EXTRA TOUCHES FOR YOUR GUEST ROOM

- These days, most people travel with laptops, cell phones, tablets, or other electronic devices. To make your guests feel at home while answering their email or posting pictures of their adventures, be sure there is comfortable access to an outlet in the room, perhaps near a small desk that can double as a nightstand. Also, leave a welcome card with the WiFi code for easy internet access.

- There is nothing like getting late-night munchies after everyone has gone to bed. Create a goody basket with bottled water, healthy snacks, and possibly even some not-so-healthy snacks for your guests. This also helps those who like to be up at the crack of dawn from going hungry for several hours before you wake up. If you have space, invest in a small coffee-maker, preferably with pods for easy cleanup, a couple of coffee cups and maybe some tea bags. Place it all on a tray on the dresser or desk. This way guests can make themselves a cup at any time, especially if they are on a different schedule than yours.

- Provide an overnight kit for your guests in another small basket placed in plain view on the dresser or in the bathroom with toothbrushes, toothpaste, floss, shampoo, conditioner, liquid soaps, disposable razors, and maybe even a pretty little cosmetic case with some feminine supplies. Think of the items that are provided in a nicely appointed hotel room, or things that you sometimes forget to pack when you're on the road. The guest room is not a place for bar soap. You don't want to reuse someone's bar soap in a hotel, and your guests don't want to share with prior guests, either.

- Set out extra towels and check that spare rolls of toilet paper are easy to find. I also keep some cleaning supplies in the bathroom. A couple of clean rags, carpet cleaner, clothing spot remover, and a spray cleaner will allow your guests to discreetly clean up an accidental spill without using your best towels.

I can't emphasize enough how helpful it is to take a trial run in your guest bedroom. You will discover so much that will help you when your guests arrive. It gives you the opportunity to work out any kinks and make last-minute additions. The more preplanning you do, the more enjoyable the experience will be for everyone when you have guests in your home.

BATHROOMS MADE BEAUTIFUL

If your dream bathroom is expansive and spa-like, and your *now* bathroom is tiny and dark, you can, at a bare minimum, confirm that everything functions as you'd expect—from the fixtures to the ventilation. The bathroom is one place where you can demonstrate every day how you care about yourself, no matter what it looks like. But you can make a small bathroom beautiful by making the right selections.

ACCESSORIZING

Have fun with your accessories! This is where you can let your personality shine, but you don't need many of them. Towels do double duty for function and design; try coordinating them with other accents in the room—a bath mat, a soap dispenser, a wastebasket, and the shower curtain, if you have one. At a minimum, choose a color that doesn't clash with the rest of your décor. No surprise, my towels are white. I also like to keep a white robe right next to the shower.

If you have a shiny countertop, choose a soap dispenser in a contrasting matte finish or something with a texture. If your countertop is a matte finish, the juxtaposition of a shiny soap dispenser would look more interesting.

WALL COLOR

First, choose a wall color that complements your skin tone. Choose something you love to see surrounding your entire face and body each day, as you view yourself in the mirror. A mustard tone or an overly bright color might not do your skin justice. Some colors can also skew your makeup and clothing choices. I once designed a professional makeup room for a TV studio in New York; the wall color was as important as the lighting. Light tones tend to work better in a bathroom, as you can see what you have to work with. However, a powder room can provide a great opportunity for a more dramatic color, as they're not often used for getting ready.

The second deciding factor in color is taking cues from your Bathroom Vision Board. Even if you only have one small bathroom right now, a Vision Board can guide your selections and make it so much easier to pull the room together.

Choose a color tone that coordinates and contrasts nicely with your hard surfaces: countertops, flooring, and shower walls. You can also pull an inspiration color from your accessories. The good news is that bathrooms are usually small and easy to repaint if you get tired of the wall color.

Choose a washable wall finish that can hold up to moisture. In a large bathroom with good ventilation, eggshell paint works well. However, if you have a small bathroom with poor ventilation, or small kids with sticky fingers, a satin finish tends to hold up better. Functional bathrooms with showers are not the best place to use wallpaper. The steam acts like a steam wallpaper remover, and the panels will roll off the wall in no time. Limit wallpaper use to powder rooms.

Flat paint is used on ceilings, but not in bathrooms where moisture pools from the shower. If the steam from your shower goes up, choose a durable finish for your ceiling paint.

FAUCETS AND FIXTURES

I am frequently asked if you can mix metals in a bathroom. The answer is yes, but the overall look is best when you coordinate your faucets, showerhead, towel bars, and cabinet hardware all in the same metal, and then contrast it with a different metal on the accessories. This gives your bathroom more of a spa like feel. Pay a little extra for a sink faucet that feels good in your hands, since you will be using it many times every day. It's a small but important gift you can give yourself. Splurge a little with your showerhead. Get something with a water pattern that feels good on your skin. Many plumbing fixture stores now have try-it-before-you-buy-it areas where you actually get to test the water flow of the showerhead.

When deciding on a glass shower door versus a shower curtain, your budget rules. However, there are some other factors to consider. When choosing a shower-door height for a standard shower, allow plenty of room for steam to escape: at least 24 inches lower than your ceiling height and no lower than your showerhead. Do you want a steam shower? If so, choose glass that extends all the way up to the ceiling and tile that completely covers the shower area, including the ceiling. If not, your ceiling sheetrock will bubble and tear in no time.

STORAGE

It seems there is never enough storage in a bathroom, so in order to reduce clutter, remember that less is more! Bathrooms accumulate half-full bottles of cleaning products, old makeup, lotions, and hair products; gift soaps we never use; all sorts of odd samples and products. Clean it all out. If you haven't opened the bottle in the last six months or so, truly, you don't want to use it now. Even in the cleanest bathrooms, everything that is out in the open attracts germs, dust, and is one more thing to clean. Keep your life simpler and healthier. Hide toothbrushes, and keep only the essentials on your counter. Medicine cabinets are great for this purpose.

Feel free to store your towels right out in the open. A basket on the floor works well for bath towels and a small basket on the counter works great for washcloths. Plus the texture of a basket adds a nice warming touch to bathrooms.

Invest in low-cost drawer organizers. Your makeup and toiletries will thank you, not to mention that you will save time. No more digging for products that should be readily available and easily found.

If space is at an extreme minimum in your bathroom, over-the-toilet storage units are available with legs that don't require attachment to the wall. Or if you're in a home where nail and screw holes don't matter, you can install floating shelves right to the wall. Invest in baskets to put on the shelves so whatever you're storing doesn't start to look like clutter.

LIGHTING

I've said this before: no one looks good with overhead lighting; it's not flattering. The harsh shadows make it hard to get your makeup and hair right. If you can, add lighting at the sides of the mirror, with sconces. If you're renting, try two tall lamps on either side of the sink, or an illuminated makeup mirror. Better bathroom lighting makes a big difference. Experiment to find the type of lightbulb that gives you the color and intensity you like. You are so worth it!

WINDOW TREATMENTS

The bathroom requires window treatments that provide complete privacy. Sheer treatments might obscure the view during the day, but they leave nothing to the imagination once darkness falls and your bathroom lights turn on. Horizontal blinds work well for maximum flexibility. You can tilt them to allow daylight in, or close them completely when you need more privacy. Vinyl blinds tend to hold up best in the damp environment of your bathroom, and they have come such a long way. Chances are that at first glance you won't be able to tell the difference between wood and plastic.

REMOVING THE YUCK

Barring a total remodel, there are plenty of ways to improve your *now* bathroom. Clean is a must. It's worth doing whatever you can do to eliminate mold, mildew, and leaks. Something as common as a malfunctioning faucet, a toilet that never shuts off, stained grout or walls, or a clogged drain in the shower isn't confidence inspiring during your most personal and private human moments. It's not a healthy atmosphere, either. A clean bathroom represents a clean human being. You deserve such a space.

12

Troubleshooting, Tweaks, and Finishing Touches

Trust yourself.
You know more than you think you do.

Benjamin Spock

What if you're close to having everything done, and it's not quite the look you expected? It's not feeling the same as those amazing photos you've been viewing on your Dream Home Vision Board all this time. You're not getting that intuitive feeling you get when you walk into a room that just feels right or finished. Then what? What do you do?

First of all, know that setbacks and second-guessing yourself along the way are normal. It's all part of the process. You'll figure it out. Sometimes it might take a few days of thinking; be patient and you will get it. And truly, nothing is ever done, nor is it ever perfect! You might even change your mind a little.

I'm always rearranging things because I suddenly find a better way or want to try something new.

Probably the number one call I get from potential clients is them saying, "My home doesn't feel right. We walked into so-and-so's home and saw what you did. Can you make our home feel like that?" Or, "We're stuck. We tried this on our own and it's not coming together. Can you fix it for us?" These feelings and experiences are all quite common. These new clients didn't have this book at their fingertips, so I would go over and "fix" their home. Now you have all the necessary tools, so you won't need me to make a house call; you can do it all on your own!

When your room isn't feeling quite right, this chapter is a checklist for troubleshooting and fine-tuning what might be missing or askew. I'll offer suggestions on how to fix the most common problems you'll encounter. It might be a case of one thing needing to be dialed in, or it might be a combination of minor issues.

After you've been away from your home for a while, clear your mind and come back, approaching your home as if you've never seen it before. With soft eyes, walk in and spend a few moments *just be*-ing, experience your home or room with all your senses, doing your Yoga Nidra.

OVERALL

Does your room have a focal point? In a gathering room, the focus should be the fireplace or a beautiful armoire or media center with a TV. Or perhaps a beautiful view. In the dining room, the table is the focus, and in a bedroom the bed should be the highlight. For the kitchen? The range and hood should star. You get the idea!

What do you see? What movements are your eyes making throughout the room. Are they zipping around, back and forth, or lingering on one piece? Is the color scheme bland, with no accents? Or is everything too bold with splashes of bright color everywhere? Do you have enough accessories, or not enough? Are you missing a desirable piece of furniture, such as a coffee table?

What do you smell, hear, feel, taste, and experience with your sixth sense? What's not quite right? A too-powerfully scented candle or something musty? A light-bulb buzzing? Scratchy fabrics? Or what else?

AT THE GROUND LEVEL

Is the room feeling too airy, almost like it's floating away? You might be missing grounding elements at the floor. The color might not be balanced on the ground with what is happening higher up in the room. Is the carpet the same light neutral color as the walls? This makes everything dark pop out at you, and not always in a cohesive way. An area rug is helpful in bringing your colors to the ground level. An area rug will also tie together your furniture, and reinforce a seating group. Make sure all your furniture isn't pushed up against the walls. And is all the furniture leggy? You might need to add an upholstered piece or two with fabric all the way to the floor. If every piece of furniture is on visible legs, it can start to feel like an office waiting room.

MID LEVEL

Is the room feeling flat and uninteresting? You might be missing color at the mid level. Try switching out decorative pillows, lampshades, coffee-table books, or throw blankets to bring in some of the color tones from your area rug or artwork.

You might need a plant at the center of the coffee table to pull in the green tones if you have a single tree in the corner. If most of your colors are light, add some darker tones for interest, but not too dark as to be busy or distracting.

EYE LEVEL

Is your room feeling heavy? You might have all the color, texture, and interest too low, weighted at the ground and mid level, with little of interest at the eye level. Or maybe everything is too dark. Do you need more artwork? Or artwork that brings in some of the color tones from the items below it? You might need a tall tree to add color and texture at a higher level.

What about draperies? Adding fabric at the window level that coordinates with other colors in the room can pull things together, even if it's a tonal fabric the same color as the sofa. The texture along the windows can also serve to visually warm a room.

Are the ceilings too tall? Add a chandelier or other light fixture in the center of the room. Or, in a bedroom, a canopy bed. This helps humanize the space by lowering the ceilings.

Are your ceilings too low? This is harder to resolve, especially if your room is big. Pull your furniture in from the walls. Tall plants in the corners work for low ceilings too, and so do floor lamps. Have your draperies go all the way from the ceiling to the floor.

RIBBONING

Next look around your room as if it were a circle. Is the color evenly distributed around the room? Or is all the color loaded up on one side of the room? A good rule of thumb when it comes to color balance is to use each color at least three times. Check that you've ribboned your colors not only from bottom to top, but that they are also ribboned in a circular motion all the way around the room.

FURNITURE PLACEMENT

For a welcoming look, arrange the seating area to be slightly open to the entry of a room, like open arms! *If the room is feeling cold*, you might have the seating pieces spread too far apart, or pointed in opposite directions, sort of like people in an elevator. Furniture represents people; make it a party, not an elevator! And if you have more than one seating area, each should function on its own, with some good space between them.

Is the room feeling cramped or cluttered? Maybe everything is too close together. Try removing a piece or two, and open up the arrangement. Give yourself some breathing room. If it feels cluttered you might also have too many small items. Your bookcases might be too full or you might have too many end tables. Try reducing the number of surfaces.

ACCESSORIES

Do you still have objects in your room that you don't love, that you're forcing to work? Do one more check and get real with yourself. Are you holding on to an item that no longer looks good with your new aesthetic or purchases? Are you keeping it because you spent big bucks on it, or it was a gift? If so, do yourself and your room a favor, and take the item to add to your giveaway pile. Do you have accessories for the sake of having accessories? Shelves can quickly turn into clutter magnets. Remember, less is more. Just like with your wardrobe, do one last look and remove a piece before you leave the house, or in this case, the room. Your original cleaning-out giveaway pile should be long gone and not sitting around collecting dust, so start a new giveaway pile. This process of cleaning up and clearing out need not end.

LIGHT QUALITY

Is your room too bright? Our living room had an odd color tone at nighttime. It turned out that we had way too much light from the chandeliers overhead. We couldn't even dim them down far enough. Everything was just too bright. With only overhead lighting, nothing looks its best. Taking down one chandelier, thus cutting the number of lightbulbs in half, made a huge difference. It still wasn't quite enough, though. We needed to add accent lighting at the mid level, including lamps on the sofa table. We also added accent lighting in the form of uplights behind two crystals sitting on shelves

to each side of the fireplace. Those simple fixes did the trick, and now I love our living room at night.

Pay attention to the light quality in your room. Do your lightbulbs need to be warmed up, or whitened up? Lower or higher wattage? Do you need to add another layer of accent lighting for dimension and interest? Lighting plays a bigger role in how your home feels than you could ever imagine.

KEEPING IT ALL IN PERSPECTIVE

It's easy to judge before the entire room is complete. Unless you have extremely good visual skills and can see the room in your head long before it's done, don't get too nervous about the overall look and feel. Wait until you're finished with the entire room plan—every piece. Then check all of the areas listed above. If you still have a few items left to complete, that could be the magic that pulls the entire thing together for you.

When my team and I design homes for clients, we strongly prefer to have a move-in day where we install everything at once. We keep a storage unit until every last item arrives, and then have a big reveal day for the client. This gives us a chance to fine-tune and allows them to see the entire look at once, with fresh eyes. When we don't do it this way, when we deliver piece by piece, disappointment sometimes crops up along the way, as it's easy for the person who lives in the partially finished home on a daily basis to lose perspective of the entire vision.

In your home, unless you have a large budget now, it might be difficult to pull off a big reveal for yourself all at once. So try to keep things in perspective as the room starts to take shape. It's like growing out your hair; not all stages look good as you're working toward your dream home.

Keep the faith that you hold the tools and the talent to pull this off. If you need to, flip back through previous chapters and reread some of the design tips.

Keep the faith that you hold the tools and the talent to pull this off. If you need to, flip back through previous chapters and reread some of the design tips. Feel free to go back as needed and check the advice against how you actually phased in your projects. Did you start with a Vision Board? Did you establish your intention? Are you working your way through your Projects List? If so, review the various phases, especially cleaning up and clearing out. Re-evaluate all elements that affect your six senses. Reread the eleven Designer's Secrets behind creating a room (see chapter 9). Then do a balance check from ground level to mid level to eye level. If you do these things, you'll catch what's feeling off and bring things back on track.

WHEN IT'S NOT FEELING QUITE RIGHT, DON'T GIVE UP HOPE! GO THROUGH THE FOLLOWING CHECKLIST:

- Soften your eyes to get the overall picture.

- Tune in to all of your senses.

- Evaluate the ground level, mid level, and eye level.

- Do colors ribbon, and are they balanced?

- Is the furniture placement functional and comfortable?

- Do you have appealing, coordinated accessories?

- Is the light quality as desired?

You Deserve Your Dream Home Now

Whatever you can do or dream, you can. Begin it!
Boldness has genius, power, and magic in it!

Widely attributed to Goethe

We've been through quite a journey together! It's with much emotion that I write my conclusion. My biggest hope is that you realize that no matter where you came from, and no matter where you are in your life right now, you deserve to have your dream home just as much as anyone else in this world.

You hold the power to make this happen, and you can choose from this day forward to take action and make the home you have *now* a place you *love coming home* to.

Home is your base. Home is your sanctuary. It's where your best life begins. If you take the time to make your home environment what it needs to be in order for you and your family to thrive, this strong base will support all aspects of your life. Whether your home is rented, shared, or owned, make it your priority to create an environment that will support everything you aspire to. Your home, the space you occupy, is yours. It's not your neighbor's home, nor your mom's, your coworker's, or your friend's. You deserve a home that truly embraces your individuality and the way you want to live. Every aspect of your home should make you smile.

Dream big! Dream as big as you possibly can. Coming from humble beginnings in a tiny country town, cleaning other people's homes, picking berries, and holding odd jobs, I never imagined that I'd one day have the life and home that I have now. I feel so fortunate to be able to live in a home that I love, one that suits me to my core. None of this happened by accident. I made a conscious decision to make my home, and my home life, a mission. I started with a hope of something more, and through the power of a Vision Board, that dream home became reality.

It wasn't always easy. Throughout my own journey, I struggled with self-doubt and fear. Sometimes I'd stray off course, thinking I was dreaming way too big, doubting that I was worthy. My dreams seemed so far away from how I was then living. Doubt crept in along the way, but I would look at my Dream Home Vision Board and realize that it was possible for someone, anyone, so why not me?

For challenging times, one of my favorite sayings is: Action conquers fear.

For challenging times, one of my favorite sayings is: Action conquers fear. It is so true. It took reflection, planning, and hard work, but it was somehow inspiring and liberating to know that it was my responsibility to take the steps I needed to move forward. It gave me the courage to go beyond my fears and realize that through my actions and intentions I could achieve my dreams. You can have this too. Start with your Vision Board. Dream big! The "What would you do if you knew you could not fail" kind of big! Pure potential.

Once you create your Dream Home Vision Board, start applying it right here and right now to your *now* home. Even if you think your *now* home isn't your dream home, it can have a number of the elements of your dream home, and it can be your launching pad to get everything you want out of life.

Start by setting your intention for your home. This is such a powerful tool. Many go through life not sure of what they want. But not you! Get clear on what you want out of your *now* home. Then set your intentions, room by room.

Clear out the clutter before you do anything else. Get rid of it! Finish your unfinished projects and piles of things that need to be thrown away, given away, or organized and put away.

Get present in your *now* home. How does it feel to all of your senses? Get clear on what you are experiencing right now in your home. Write down anything you need to fix, adjust, or correct.

Make a list of all your home priorities. This will become your Projects List. It ensures you stay focused and don't get pulled off course by spending time and energy on projects or purchases that really don't matter to you.

Once you've taken the time to dream big, set your intention, assess your current situation, and make your goals and projects list, *then* you can think about budget.

Once you establish your budget, you can roll out a plan of your priorities. Start with what matters the most to you. Remember, the majority of the ideas and tips in this book are not expensive to accomplish, so don't put off readying your home due to a limited budget. Know that this is a temporary situation, and you are well on your way to creating a place where you will flourish. And your finances will, too.

When you're ready to dive into each project, you've got a Personal Design Cheat Sheet (see Appendix) to guide you, and chapters full of design and function information at your fingertips. Apply what you have learned to each specific room in your home, and feel confident that the result will work from a design standpoint, while expressing your individuality

Be prepared to work hard, as you would to achieve any goal in life. Anything worth doing takes effort and perseverance. You will undoubtedly encounter challenges and setbacks, but these are only bumps on the road to your destination. They are a normal part of the process.

Go to gratitude when you need a pick-me-up along the way. Think of all you've accomplished in life and in your home thus far. Gratitude is a potent motivator.

Also, be prepared to have a great deal of fun along the way. You are in the process of creating your dream home. A home where you will thrive! Celebrate the successes and finished projects. Toast with a glass of champagne or anything else that equals a celebratory moment for you. Don't let these moments of reward slip away.

You deserve a home you *love coming home* to. You can do this. Your best life starts at home!

Acknowledgments

I am immensely grateful to all of the many mentors, who have taught me so much in design and in life. Their support and inspiration have seen me through to this point in life.

If it weren't for my inspiring publishers, Richard Cohn and Michele Ashtiani Cohn, and their dedicated team, this book would not have been written. You saw potential and encouraged me to write from my heart. This book is a dream come true. Thank you!

Emily Han, my incredibly talented editor, thank you for your detailed focus to every single word in this book! Your guidance, creative solutions, and thoughtful feedback are the glue and the magic that this book needed.

Lindsay Brown, and her team at Beyond Words Publishing, thank you for setting a design vision, and bringing to life such a beautiful, strategically laid out, and well designed book, from cover to interior. Not to mention, ensuring every word had reason for staying in the book. You are so talented and dedicated, and I am very fortunate to have you on my team. Who would have thought . . . you use Vision Boards for a book cover, too!

Elaine Bothe, thank you for reading my book in its raw form, and for continually giving constructive feedback and making meaningful contributions along the way.

Bri Garbani, thank you for collaborating on the aesthetic vision for my book.

If it weren't for Costco and their invitation to join their Journey's family as a speaker, I would not have been in the right place at the right time. So for this, I thank Ginnie Roeglin, Diane Tieske, and Sue McConnaha.

And lastly, but most importantly, thank you to my dream-come-true husband, JR Meyers, for all of your patience and support during the late nights and long weekends of writing. I had you on my Vision Board for years, but you are so much better in real life than I ever could have imagined!

Your Personal Design Cheat Sheet

Here is a quick guide you can refer to when putting together your design plan for any room in your home:

1. Room name

2. What is the purpose and intention for this room?

- How do you want to use this room?

- Is there an activity you want to do in this room that you can't do anywhere else in your home?

- Ideally, how many people do you want to have in this room at any one time?

- How do you want to feel in this room? How do you want others to feel here? What is the mood you want to set?

3. *Expand your vision. Create a new Vision Board for this particular room.*

- If you're using some of the same images as on your Dream Home Vision Board, make a copy first.

- Watch for recurring themes on your board that will help you make your furniture-purchasing decisions.

- What arm, feet, and body styles are you seeing on the pieces on your board?

- What wood tones and fabric colors do you notice?

4. *What is your budget?*

- What can you DIY?

- What tasks do you need help with? Get two or three bids before hiring out any of the work.

- What purchases need to be made? Pre-shop and add the prices or price ranges to your budget spreadsheet before making any purchases.

- Can you find extra cash by selling existing home furnishings that no longer serve a purpose in your home?

- Set your priorities based on what your budget will allow.

5. *Set your timeline!*

- Determine a time frame for completing your Room Vision Board.

- Think about your Projects List. Is there an event by when you want this room done? Put each project and purchase on your schedule.

- Are there repairs that need to happen? Any remodeling planned? Get quotes in advance.

- Establish your budget.

- When will you move your furniture out of the room and clean your area rugs?

- Paint.

- Clean or replace carpets.

- Move furniture back into the room.

- Fine-tune, and adjust your accessories.

- Enjoy your hard work!

6. *Create your space plan and furniture layout.*

- Draw your room, including windows, doors, openings, and immovable features (fireplaces, built-in shelves, and so on).
    - ◈ What is the primary focal point of this room?

- Lay out your furniture—large pieces first.

- Add your accent furniture.

- Area rugs

7. *Establish your palette.*

- Fabrics

- Paint

8. *Last additions and purchases.*

- What items can you repurpose, and what can you toss?

- Accessories:
  - ◈ Art
  - ◈ Mirrors
  - ◈ Rugs
  - ◈ Candles
  - ◈ Books
  - ◈ Treasures
  - ◈ Throw pillows and blankets
  - ◈ Plants
  - ◈ Window treatments
  - ◈ Lamps

Notes

1. *UT News* (University of Texas at Austin), press release, "Adm. McRaven Urges Graduates to Find Courage to Change the World," May 16, 2014, https://news.utexas.edu/2014/05/16/mcraven-urges-graduates-to-find -courage-to-change-the-world.

2. Steve Bradt, "Wandering Mind Not a Happy Mind," *Harvard Gazette*, November 11, 2010, https://news.harvard.edu/gazette/story/2010/11 /wandering-mind-not-a-happy-mind/.

3. Martha J. Nepper, "The Relationships between the Home Food Environment and Weight Status among Children and Adolescents, Ages 6–17 Years." abstract (PhD diss., University of Nebraska–Lincoln, 2016), https://digitalcommons.unl.edu/nutritiondiss/61/.

4. Eckhart Tolle, *The Power of Now: A Guide to Spiritual Enlightenment* (Novato, CA: New World Library, 1997), 56.

5. Eckhart Tolle, *Practicing the Power of Now: Essential Teachings, Meditations, and Exercises from "The Power of Now"* (Novato, CA: New World Library, 1999), 52.

6. Rhonda Byrne, *The Magic* (New York: Atria Books, 2012), 146.

7. Scott Barry Kaufman, "The Real Neuroscience of Creativity," *Scientific American*, August 19, 2013, https://blogs.scientificamerican.com /beautiful-minds/the-real-neuroscience-of-creativity/.

8. "Observation Skills May be Key Ingredient to Creativity," Association for Psychological Science, June 26, 2014, https://www.psychologicalscience.org/news/minds-business/observation-skills-may-be-key-ingredient-to-creativity.html.

9. Thorin Klosowski, "How to Boost Your Observation Skills and Learn to Pay Attention," *Life Hacker*, January 8, 2015, https://lifehacker.com/how-to-boost-your-observation-skills-and-learn-to-pay-a-1678229721.

10. Dr. Greg Cason, in conversation with author, December 2, 2017.

11. Dr. Greg Cason, in conversation with author, December 2, 2017.

12. Jack Canfield, "Making Way for Success through Task Completion," *Jack Canfield* (blog), accessed on January 6, 2018, http://jackcanfield.com/blog/the-cycle-of-completion-making-way-for-success/.

13. Canfield, "Making Way for Success," *Jack Canfield* (blog).

14. Suze Orman, "5 Ways to Keep Remodeling Costs Down," Oprah.com, accessed January 6, 2018, http://www.oprah.com/money/remodeling-a-home-for-less-money-suze-ormans-advice.

15. Suze Orman, "The Cheapest Way to Go Green," Oprah.com, accessed January 6, 2018, http://www.oprah.com/money/suze-ormans-guide-to-making-low-cost-eco-upgrades/all#ixzz4znCXelX9.

16. Midwest Plan Service, *The House Handbook: Guidelines for Building or Remodeling Your Home* (Ames: Iowa, MidWest Plan Services, Iowa State University, 2016), 51.

17. Kitty Lascurain, "Nursery Color Psychology: Let Science Decide," thespruce.com, October 11, 2017, https://www.thespruce.com/color-psychology-for-kids-2504750.

18. Crystal Bonser, "How to Design a Nursery Which Would Stimulate the Intellectual Development of a Child," LiveStrong.com, June 13, 2017, https://www.livestrong.com/article/560169-how-to-design-a-nursery-which-would-stimulate-the-intellectual-development-of-a-child/.

About the Author

Jennifer Adams is an award-winning designer, author, and TV personality whose passion for calm, mindful living encourages others to do so with the same authenticity. Every day, Jennifer works to create high-quality yet attainable products that reflect her own Southern California easy, breezy, effortless style, believing everyone deserves to have a space they love coming home to. Her creativity, content expertise, media presence, and recent graduation from Harvard Business School under the OPM Program for entrepreneurship have all contributed to the continued growth of her business, Home by Jennifer Adams®. And, even more is yet to come!